CW01083069

About the Author

Scott Manson was born in Paisley, Scotland, and immigrated to Sydney, Australia, with his family, in 1966. After several moves between migrant hostels, his family settled in the northwest suburb of Dundas. He had planned to become a meteorologist after leaving High School, but a change in the minimum age requirement from 18 to 21 years meant he found work in a different direction, the travel industry, and had never looked back.

Despite loving the Australian flora and fauna, he couldn't settle, and in 1991 returned to his native town of Paisley, where he resumed his career in travel.

This book is dedicated to my son Blair.
He would often ask, "Where is Dad off to now?"

END-TO-END

The World's Longest Train Journey

Vila Real de Santo Antonio, Portugal
to
Ho Chi Minh City, Vietnam

This journey was completed in September 2019. A couple of months later it's thought someone got way too close to a bat in a wet market in Wuhan, China, and the rest, as they say, is history – and sadly still in the making.

CONTENTS

IN THE BEGINNING...

Itchy feet, the travel bug, wanderlust or hodophilia. You name it, I suffer from it – and always have.

I recall, when in high school in the 1970s, I would study the green expanse of the USSR in my school atlas. Small regions called Latvia, Lithuania, Estonia and White Russia looked like little countries, but seemed to be part of the Soviet Union, all coloured the same shade of green. The word 'annexation' had not yet entered my vocabulary. I found a thin black line, crossing the USSR, from Moscow to Vladivostok, and discovered references to the Trans-Siberian Railway in the school library. While my friends read books such as Silas Marner, I conducted feasibility studies on crossing the communist Motherland. No wonder I didn't fit in.

Fast forward twenty years and my 'list of things to do' had been created, years before 'bucket lists' had been invented. The term originated as recently as 2007 from the film 'The Bucket List'. My list contained list of goals to complete before shuffling off my mortal coil. As I loved to read, a friend of a friend once offloaded around 50 copies of Reader's Digest onto me. I grudgingly accepted them, not wishing to appear rude or ungrateful. In one edition, an article suggested the creation of a 'Things to do before you die' list, and I was suitably inspired.

Bizarrely, years later in Canada, while enjoying a pleasant business lunch at Niagara-on-the-Lake, I mentioned this article to a colleague. Visiting Niagara Falls and experiencing a helicopter ride appeared on my 'list'. My colleague proceeded to dig into the depths of her handbag, and pulled out the same article, the creased, dog-eared pages torn from the same Reader's Digest edition. I love coincidences, but they also make me feel uneasy, as if I'm starring in my own version of The Truman Show, with these surprises designed to generate an entertaining reaction.

Remember the thin, black line? How far could I travel if the black line continued through Mongolia and into China. What about at the other end, through Eastern and onto Western Europe? From end-to-end, how long would be needed to complete the longest train journey on the planet, and also, how feasible would such a journey be? More importantly, why would anyone, in their right mind, want to take such a journey? I blame it on my itchy feet, the travel bug, wanderlust or hodophilia.

By 2010 my financial situation had improved, and I also had the courage and inclination to carry out such a trip. Over the years I had been fortunate enough to travel by train across large swathes of Western Europe, from Hamburg to Naples, from Vienna to Bordeaux. I asked myself "What's the worst that could happen when train-hopping halfway around the world?" I would wait another nine years to find out, and for me to complete the journey of a lifetime.

The Trans-Siberian Railway may be the longest single train route in the world, but this isn't the longest journey by train. Follow the thin black line across Russia, through Mongolia and onto Beijing, Shanghai, across the Vietnamese border and on to Ho Chi Minh City and the black line will abruptly end. In the other direction, the black line snakes west to Minsk, Warsaw, Berlin, Paris and Lisbon, and eventually fizzles out by the Spanish border at Vila Real de Santo Antonio in the Algarve region.

This journey had a set of straightforward rules; no zigzags, no unnecessary deviations and use only the most logical, direct route. With the simple ground rules settled, the distance from Vila Real de Santo Antonio to Ho Chi Minh City was calculated to be a mere 18,296 kilometres or 11,368 miles. This journey would involve 23 trains and take 35 days. The distance could be covered much quicker, but considering the exotic cities I would pass through, it would be senseless not to spend at least two nights (one full day) at most of the connection points.

GETTING TO VILA REAL DE SANTO ANTONIO

I flew to Faro, Portugal with Jet2, on a noisy flight. Excited holidaymakers filled the aircraft, with a stag party group ensuring the onboard noise levels were kept high. A couple of the cabin crew also joined in the party atmosphere. The flight arrived 30 minutes early and with a sigh of relief my backpack appeared on the luggage carrousel ahead of the other 188 passengers. Having my luggage lost would have put a serious dampener on the whole trip. In fact the journey may have ended before it even started. I managed to walk through the airport and out of the front door of the terminal building in just a few minutes, well ahead of the crowd behind me. A blast of warm air reminded me this wasn't a holiday, but the start of a most challenging adventure. However, I still had to find my way to the starting point.

I never seem to stroll up to a bus stop with just a few minutes to wait before a bus arrives, but instead seem to just *miss* a bus by a few minutes. Predictably, I missed a bus by five minutes and based on the timetable displayed, there would be a 30-minute wait for the next one. This effectively wiped out any time gained by my speedy passage through the airport. Guaranteed the next bus would not arrive on time. Waiting at a bus stop seems to make time pass slower. Stephen Hawking claimed black holes had a dramatic effect on time, slowing it down far more than anything else in the galaxy. Perhaps his inspiration came one day while waiting for a bus at Faro Airport in the Portuguese sun.

Eventually the bus to Faro city centre arrived, albeit 20 minutes late, followed by a free-for-all of tired, hot and impatient humanity attempting to squeeze through the door all at once.
I don't enjoy buses. They leave from bus stops. One bus stop looks like any other bus stop. Can I be 100% sure this is the right bus stop, and guarantee the bus will actually stop? Bus stops only show the final destination, and not intermediate stops, unlike display boards at railway stations.

Trains, on the other hand, run on tracks, on a predictable route, and are easy to spot. Trains stop at large buildings called stations and have long platforms. I don't enjoy buses. Once in the town centre, I boarded the railcar to Vila Real de Santo Antonio, smug in the knowledge no buses would be used for the next 35 days.

DAY 0:
VILA REAL DE SANTO ANTONIO, PORTUGAL

I decided to get acclimatised, soak up a little vitamin D and walk to the nearest beach. Praia da Ponta da Areia lay just two miles south of the town centre, but the walk felt more like twenty-two. Maritime Pines flanked the road to the beach, but they offered little shade, and the heat bounced off the roads and pavements. Today's temperature would hit the mid-30s Celsius, and soon realised I had brought insufficient water with me. The road to Hell ran parallel to the Guadiana River. In the middle of the river lay a sandbar, about 500 metres long, with seven small boats beached. Visitors to the island made the most of the low tide and their own private strip of sand.

This stretch of riverbank, and the stone breakwater, which jutted into the Atlantic Ocean, were popular locations with fishermen. A dozen men stood in the sun, all overweight, with their guts hanging over the elastic on their shorts, and all well tanned. These men seemed content to spend their day achieving little, waiting for their lines to tug, and appeared to be catching nothing apart from skin cancer. Previous fishermen had left their mark with a trail of litter; beer bottles, empty bait boxes and lengths of tangled fishing line. One man, also overweight, wearing shorts and well suntanned, stood up to his knees in the water, looking for crabs to use as bait. He also didn't seem to be having much luck.

Several hundred vacationers were enjoying the beach. Only a dozen could be seen splashing in the surf, with all others lying on towels in the shade under colourful umbrellas. To be honest, I wasn't sure what might be lurking in the Atlantic Ocean off the Praia da Ponta da Areia.

My upbringing in Sydney would expose me to many beach hazards, and the worst one without teeth, was the nasty Portuguese man o' war, also commonly called a bluebottle. We referred to this monster as a jellyfish, but technically it was siphonophore. Either way, the Portuguese man o' war was a beast best avoided.

If the name didn't cause concern, the threat of a painful sting

11

would. The potent sting was powerful enough to kill fish and the occasional human splashing around in the surf. With tentacles around 10 metres or 30 feet in length, these nasty bastards must be avoided at all costs. The name "man o' war" comes from the man-of-war, an 18th-century sailing warship, and because the creature resembled the Portuguese caravel at full sail. Many years ago, a fragment of tentacle once touched my chest while I splashed about at Manly beach, north of Sydney. The intense pain ensured my afternoon seaside visit came to an abrupt end. It's been said having someone pee on the sting can ease the pain. I found no volunteers, but made a few new friends.

Most Men o' wars are found in tropical and subtropical waters, but they have been known to float along, aided by winds and surface currents, all the way to Portugal. I later read this had been a bad season for sightings along the Algarve, which possibly explained the lack of swimmers.

One good point about Vila Real de Santo Antonio was its ease in which to leave the place. A small ferry crossed the River Guadiana to Ayamonte, on the opposite bank. At EUR3.60 return, this cheap and cheerful international ferry gave me an opportunity to visit Spain, albeit very briefly. My overnight train from Lisbon would travel through Spain to Hendaye in France without stopping, and I possibly wouldn't have an opportunity to set foot in the country. Most visitors off my ferry congregated around the main square of Plaza de la Laguna, content on either shopping or enjoying a cool drink in the shade. Naturally, I was the odd one out.

I explored the old town, perched on a hill behind the harbour. Heat bounced off the whitewashed houses and the humidity and lack of air movement soon became oppressive. The picturesque, whitewashed, 16th century Capilla de San Antonio sat empty, except for a man sweeping the floor. Only a crazy tourist would be silly enough to walk through the narrow, cobbled, deadly quiet streets and battle the summer heat and humidity.

After a few wrong turns, the town's bullring loomed in front of me. I expected the building to be closed, so wasn't surprised when I found the doors securely bolted shut. Although I don't agree with this 'sport', bullfighting was ingrained in Spanish culture, and it wasn't going away

12

any time soon. The grand, whitewashed Mirador del Gurugu, dated from 1852 and was still in use, in particular during the festivities in honour of Our Lady of Sorrows held each September. I really hoped to have a peek inside somehow, but found every door shut tighter than a matador's pants.

Back in Portugal, I had to visit the buffer stop at the end of the line, about 350 metres beyond Vila Real de Santo Antonio railway station. As a symbolic gesture, a random piece of granite ballast was chosen to carry to the buffer stop at the other end of the line at Ho Chi Minh City. I slid the stone carefully into my backpack as it had a long way to go.

DAY 1:
VILA REAL DE SANTO ANTONIO– LISBON

I took a shortcut to the station by walking down a dusty track, and through a glade of whispering eucalyptus trees. For a brief moment I was transported back to Australia and back in time thirty years. The trees reminded me of how much I missed the Australian flora, which played an important part of my growing up down under. My Aussie reminisces became complete when a swarm of black flies attacked me, landing on my face, my arms, in my ears and in my mouth. After all those years, the Great Aussie Salute came back so naturally - the movement of the hand in brushing away flies.

Vila Real de Santo Antonio would definitely be the quietest station on this entire journey. I stood on the platform, admiring the stunning, white Art Deco station building, and how it contrasted with the multi-coloured graffitied, stainless steel railcar bound for Faro. For a few moments I wondered if I would be the only passenger on this train until, at the last moment, other passengers began to arrive. Regular users were aware of the train times and were comfortable strolling up a few minutes before departure. I had arrived early, with time to spare, but then again, I was the only passenger bound for Vietnam and didn't want to miss my first train.

Graffiti covered the outside of the railcar, preventing clear views. The railcar was non-air-conditioned, and as expected, the windows wouldn't open. Thank goodness this uncomfortable journey would only be about an hour in length.

As most of my recent train travel involved commuting to and from Glasgow Central station, I found the Algarve and the abrupt change of scenery fascinating. The parched landscape featured eucalyptus trees, scrawny cacti, salt pans, and what appeared to be the occasional abandoned, withered vineyard. The Tavira region of Algarve produces some famous red and white wines with a high alcohol content. I tend to stay clear of wines, as one glass sees me sliding down under – under the table.

14

Our train grew busier at Porta Nova. Three Germans boarded: the husband and wife sat on one side of the aisle, and the other man sat opposite me. I came to the conclusion these men were German, before they even opened their mouths. They looked so... well, stereotypically Prussian, being overweight, in their 50s, and with white moustaches. Their topic of conversation focussed on German football, with the wife feigning interest, occasionally smiling politely. Most of her attention was directed out of the window at the dry Algarve scenery, perhaps secretly wishing for a glass or two of fine Tavira wine as a form of anesthesia.

We rattled across the dry coastal plain. Several seats along the carriage, an old woman fanned her husband sitting opposite. He leant forward and placed a hand against his forehead, struggling with the heat, which, to be honest, had become rather uncomfortable. She fanned and fanned him, but his face remained an unhealthy shade of red. Our conductor passed through the train and asked if he needed assistance, and then walked to the end of the car, unlocking two small windows. Time to step outside of my comfort zone and be the carriage hero.

"Would he like my water?" I asked, offering the woman my remaining half-bottle of water. She didn't speak English, but understood my gesture. She thanked me with an "Obrigada" and explained he just struggled with the heat. No other passengers offered to help this poor man.

Our train passed lines of olive trees, and then one exhausted goat. It sought relief from the heat, by standing in what little shade a sagging tree could offer. A poor horse stood still in the centre of a paddock in direct sunlight, its head drooped, with a white heron perched on its back. A herd of cattle fed on what little grass they could find in a parched field. The flora contrasted with my native Scotland and I found it fascinating; tangerine orchards, pomegranates, giant seedgrass, and various eucalyptus trees and shrubs.

The train passed a patch of Piteira, or American Agave, growing by a farm building. This brought back memories of my Australian childhood when we used to carve our initials into the green-grey leaves. These plants were very nasty due to their long serrated leaves and prickly margins. At the end of each leaf was a heavy spike and I could testify these hurt when you were stupid enough to lean against one. Piteira deserved to be respected.

I helped an older woman wearing a headscarf at Luz station, by lifting her mountain bike up from the low platform and up onto the train. The four-foot height difference would have been a struggle for anyone to lift a heavy mountain bike up into the carriage. I also lifted her bike down when she left the train, a few stops along the line. Again, no one else offered to help.

FARO, PORTUGAL

I had plenty of connection time at Faro, so strolled along the platform to have a closer look at two trains. At one platform sat a huge, red locomotive attached to a grimy passenger train, and at the opposite platform a sleek, high speed Pendolino waited in the sun.

A station employee named Antonio approached me, and we started up a conversation. He surprised me when he wanted to talk about the main line between London and Glasgow.

"Have you a Pendolino train on that line?" he asked.

"It's a Pendolino, but probably not as fast as your train to Lisbon."

"Why is that?"

"Our Pendolinos can hit high speeds, but the route is too twisty to reach full speed except in a few locations."

Antonio had seen a TV program about the line, and wished to speak to anyone who had travelled on these tilting trains.

He told me he was visiting Paddington station in London when a major rail accident took place. I couldn't recall the details of this accident, so researched this later. The Ladbroke Grove train crash took place on the 5th October 1999, and killed 31 people and injured more than 400.

"I phoned my brother here to tell him I was safe."

I bid him farewell and wandered down in the direction of Faro

Marina. I ordered an omelette at a restaurant called Afé do Oreto.

Today's weather was stunning, with a cloudless sky, and a warm breeze blowing off the water. Deep down I wished this weather would follow me all of the way to Ho Chi Minh City.

While relaxing and enjoying my lunch, I noticed aircraft departed from Faro Airport every five or ten minutes. Their flight path passed over the marina, and the roar of jet engines from each aircraft's departure could not be ignored. This was a reminder, to all visitors, the vacation clock was ticking, and before long we would be on an aircraft heading home - except for me. I would be sitting in a train heading into the unknown, in the direction of Vietnam.

Afé do Oreto was actually my second attempt at lunch. My first attempt took place at a small café on Avenida da República. An assortment of white plastic tables and chairs spilled out onto the pavement, with a few customers eating al fresco. After a quick look at the menu, and a reassuring grunt to myself, I sat down by a table, and waited patiently for a waiter to take an order. Howls of laughter drifted from inside the restaurant, and there seemed to be a real reluctance for anyone to come out onto the pavement and occasionally check to see if any new customers had arrived. After five minutes, my stomach told me to find another place and so headed towards the marina. Even at the Afé do Oreto patience was required, but at least staff were scurrying around and actually serving people. Waiters will only see you when they are ready to see you, and not before.

Back at Faro station, I sat in the shade of the platform canopy, waiting for the Lisbon-bound train to arrive. Three Australians, one man and two girls, all from Melbourne, sat to my right. Not realising other passengers might understand English, and even be from the United Kingdom, one girl, while munching digestive biscuits, asked the other two "Why do Poms get upset when you call them Poms? That's what they are."

I was tempted to say to her a very small number of Aussies were racist bastards, and they would object to being called that, despite actually being racist bastards.

"We met a girl when we were in New Zealand." said the second girl. "There were two ferries at the dock, and she caught the wrong one, and ended up on a random island somewhere."

I realised I had missed the link between Poms and New Zealand ferry services, when the conversation veered off on a new tangent. The first girl began to slag-off the Australian Rules football team Geelong. As a Geelong supporter, I fought hard not to make a comment. I just bit my tongue and secretly hoped she would choke on her digestive biscuits.

The Faro-Lisbon train left five minutes late, with very few passengers. This was to change at Albufeira, when backpackers filled the remaining seats. A woman, in her early 20s, occupied the vacant window seat to my left. She had piercing blue eyes, long blonde hair and denim hot pants... well, you get the picture.

Her name was Louise and came from Illinois. This would be her first visit to Lisbon, and proceeded to tell me nothing else. She may have suspected an ulterior motive for my chit-chat. Perhaps Louise thought I was writing a travel book or just bordering on being a creep.

Portugal isn't a large country. In fact the distance from north to south is roughly the same as Glasgow-London, Toronto-New York or San Francisco-Los Angeles. For those readers familiar with the United States, Portugal roughly shares the same area as Iowa or Louise's home state of Illinois. It's possible to easily cross this country from north to south in a day. My train from Faro to Lisbon wasn't a sleek Pendolino, but pulled by an aging electric locomotive, which offered a slower, but better, view of the passing scenery. However, many passengers missed the scenery by closing their lime green curtains to block out the sunshine.

Five minutes after leaving Albufeira carnage broke out around me. Imagine a group of backpackers heading single-file along the carriage looking for their seats ("Shit, we're in the wrong car!"), only to be met by another group of equally lost backpackers heading towards them. Three passengers added to the confusion by standing in the aisle between both groups struggling to read their seat reservations. A full ten minutes passed before the gridlock cleared from the car, and a sense of calm returned to the train.

Louise had nodded off while reading, so I had a sneaky glance at the book cover, 'The Girl on the Train' by Paula Hawkins. I recognised the title, but hadn't read the book, or even knew the storyline. This seemed to be a jolly good book for a girl to read on a train - until I read the subtitle: 'You don't know her, but she knows you.' Now she appeared a bit creepy. At least it wasn't '50 Shades of Grey'. As things turned out, Louise wasn't a stalker, and continued to ignore me all the way to Lisbon. I stepped off the train at Lisbon Entrecampos, and Louise stayed on board, continuing her journey to the following and final stop at Lisbon Santa Apolónia.

DAY 2:
LISBON, PORTUGAL

With a full day in Lisbon, I decided to walk to the historic 18th century Águas Livres Aqueduct. I struggled up a hill, in the beating sun, to reach a fine photo location and to capture the 65 metre high viaduct over the Alcantara Valley. An impressive online photo had been taken from a particular spot, but bushes and trees now blocked the view. Oh well. At least the sounds of dozens of chirping cicadas made up for the loss, and again memories of my Australian upbringing came flooding back.

Cicadas are amazing insects. They live in the ground for between 2 and 17 years, spending their time tunneling and eating, but not sleeping or hibernating. When ready to breed, they climb up into the trees and start chirping, and chirp some more, and some more again. A few minutes of a chirping cicada is pleasant enough. A few hours of chirping starts to become an irritation, and after several days you are thinking about dragging a garden hose over and spraying the trees to make them shut the fuck up. After a few weeks (they have a life span of 5 or 6 weeks), you start to act like Jack Nicholson in 'The Shining'.

I wondered if an aqueduct appreciation society existed. If so, this organisation would no doubt be in the UK. This country gave the world a roundabout and also pylon appreciation groups. All aqueduct devotees would be suitably impressed with Lisbon's stunning historic Águas Livres Aqueduct.

Down at the waterfront, by the Rio Tejo, I thought about visiting the iconic Belem Tower. I spotted the long line of patient visitors standing in the sun, waiting to be allowed in, before I spotted the fortification itself. There were almost 200 people waiting patiently for their opportunity to explore the interior of this iconic building. Due to the Belem Tower's historical importance, Portuguese and foreign visitors regarded this structure as a 'must see' when in Lisbon.

Belem Tower dated from the 16th century and served as a point of embarkation and disembarkation for Portuguese explorers, and also a ceremonial gateway to Lisbon. For me, Belem Tower wasn't a 'must see' attraction, but more of an 'I'd like to see' attraction, but with such a long line at the entrance, I decided I'd like to see it – some other time.

I wondered how slowly this line was moving, so used a Japanese woman in a red T-shirt and red joggers as a marker. I wandered away to photograph the tower from a few different directions and then returned after five minutes to see the line of orderly, slowly cooking visitors. She had moved just fifteen feet. At this rate I estimated it would take her over an hour to enter the tower, which was on par with Disneyworld.

Further along the shore sat the imposing Padrão dos Descobrimentos, which celebrated the Portuguese Age of Exploration during the 15th and 16th centuries. I climbed to the top for the rewarding views, and discovered the monument only dated from 1958. Why had it taken Lisboetas so long to build a monument to commemorate this great era in Portuguese history?

I also visited the Museu do Oriente, which focused on Portugal's historical links with the Far East. Unfortunately there were no displays to whet my Vietnamese appetite, as the Portuguese explorers only reached as far as Na Dang in the early 1500s, and then focussed their energy on modern-day Indonesia and China. Either way, the air conditioning was a much appreciated respite from the midday heat.

Next on my list was the Jardin Botanico d'Ajuba, which I found interesting, as small botanical gardens go. It featured flowering trees, sculptured hedges, bushes, a symmetrical layout and had the feel of a formal garden rather than a botanical garden. Unfortunately nothing remotely Vietnamese could be found. A grand eucalyptus tree grew in the garden so I wandered over for a closer look and gave this piece of Australiana a lucky pat for my journey ahead.

I made an interesting observation (okay, interesting to me) about supermarkets at Vila Real de Santo Antonio, and also now at Lisbon. Upon entering the shop, visitors were slapped in the face by the strong aroma of fish. The Portuguese love their fish, and the fish counters are at least double the size of those found at UK supermarkets. On display was a local fish called Bacalhau, a type of salted cod, sliced, laid flat, and piled high. On sale were bags of muscles, sea snails similar to whelks, and various mysterious local fish. Fish counters were decorated with fish heads complete with bulging eyes, and mouths gaping at me as I gaped back. I tried to take a photo of a Bacalhau fish mountain, but a security guard chased me.

I also noticed all small shops, which had a licence to sell alcohol, provided a table and several chairs outside. At least one customer sat outside every shop, usually a man, enjoying the shade and a cool beer. Supplementing this scene, would be the faint whiff of sewerage, wafting in the warm breeze.

DAY 3:
LISBON, PORTUGAL

I checked out of my hotel around 9am, and secured my bag in a luggage locker at Santa Apolonia Station. My train left from here tonight, so this would be the most convenient and logical option. This gave me a full day to explore more of Lisbon, although determined to take things easier than yesterday. My feet ached and wearing a sweat-soaked shirt all day had been an unpleasant experience.

My first stop was the stunning Campo Pequeno, an orange Moorish-style bullring built in 1892. Unfortunately access to the arena was forbidden, and there were no spy holes for a quick peek inside. I've never been a fan of the bull-fighting concept, and have always regarded these buildings as glorified abattoirs. However, the Campo Pequeno was indeed an impressive abattoir. Inside the building were a couple of steak restaurants, which would be like visiting an abattoir, and later tucking into a steak at the staff canteen. At least the meat would be fresh.

Another day, another botanical garden - this time the Jardin Botanic, which covered a greater area than yesterday's offering. Trees dominated this garden, and the coolness the shade provided was much appreciated. I found several plants from Japan, Korea and China, but still nothing Vietnamese. A clump of bamboo could have been Vietnamese, so decided to use my touristic licence, and declared this was close enough.

I returned to the city centre using the Lisbon Metro, and watched a blind man, carrying a cane and plastic begging cup, walk slowly along the carriage chanting. Begging was common in Lisbon, but not by the homeless, drunk or Romani type of beggar, which we see in the UK, but seemed to be beggars with physical disabilities. Anyway, the blind man managed to find his way along our carriage, when he bumped into another blind man, who also held a begging cup, heading in the opposite direction. "This will be good," I thought.

They exchanged a few comments, possibly discussing whose patch this carriage belonged to, and then both headed back to the front of the train, and continued to beg along the way in tandem. The beggars worked in cahoots with each other, using a similar technique used by ticket inspectors, who start at each end of a train and meet in the middle.

I dined outdoors on a superb paella, and washed the meal down with a Portuguese Sagres beer while conducting a little people watching. Wiping the froth from my mouth, I wondered how conspicuous I appeared, sitting here, eating and drinking on my own.

Few people seemed to be on their own. One woman, in her 40s, wearing Aztec design baggy pants, orange top and matching dyed orange hair and backpack, stood outside a souvenir shop smoking. She was dressed like a tourist, and stood out from the crowd, eventually shuffling away in the direction of Rua dos Fanqueiros.

The next single person I spotted was an overweight slob with a lazy eye, void of any fashion sense, walking along in the crowd. I hoped no one else was writing on the same subject, looking at me and scribbling in a notebook "Christ, look at the state of him." I ran my fingers through my hair, and straightened my posture just in case.

I later walked past the Elevador de Santa Justa and could not believe a line of perhaps 200 people, prepared to pay five Euros each for this lift to take them on the 45 metre ride to the top. Admittedly this was a magnificent piece of construction, but really? The elevator opened around 1899, to connect the lower streets of the Baixa with the higher Largo do Carmo. Such a long line and a long wait just to ride for 30 seconds.

Before the departure of tonight's train to Hendaye, I wasted some time by wandering around another supermarket. As the glass doors slid open, the smell of fish hit me in the face. I walked over to the fish counter, and gazed at the local dried and salted Bacalhau. The fish were laid flat, covered in salt or flour, and piled in stacks of around twenty high. I ensured my camera remained hidden, as I didn't fancy being chased by a security guard again. Photographing fish must be some sort of national security risk in Portugal. Also on display were Mexilhao (mussels) and bivalves called Lambujinha, whole squids, eels and sea snails. The fish smell was overpowering.

A friend once tried to assure me that fresh fish didn't let off any smell, and a strong smell indicated the fish was off. My argument was if

24

you visit a fish market, selling produce caught that morning, why does the place reek? It's a process of decay, but the intensity can be controlled by just washing the fish with water, or treating the fish with acidic ingredients such as lemon, vinegar, or tomato. Your average fish smell is still some way off being totally rank, unless you aren't a seafood connoisseur, and all fishy smells will give you the dry retch either way.

LISBON – HENDAYE – PARIS

I had read a report which stated a 'Grande Clas' compartment wasn't much better than a standard train compartment, so expected no "Wow!" factor. My fare entitled me to the compartment to myself, which was just as well, as the lack of storage space for a rucksack, and the limited floor space made the cabin seriously crowded.

The train lurched, and the Trenhotel began its journey from Santa Apolónia station on time. My cabin, being at the end of the carriage, entitled me to a night of bogie grunts, groans and grinds as the train wound its way through the darkness of Portugal and into Spain.

Travelling on an overnight train is both mysterious and romantic, and a sleeper cabin to myself made me deliriously happy. Overnight sleepers can turn a passenger into a sort of Peeping Tom. Our train passed houses in the dark; yellow ceiling lights illuminated living rooms and bedrooms. The occupants were seen for just a second and then judged based on that fleeting glance. They, however, were completely unaware of me, being used to the rattle of passing trains.

A German father and son occupied the compartment adjacent to me. Once the conversation and novelty of their cabin had worn off, all switches had been flicked on and off countless times, and every hinged accessory opened and closed over and over again, they succumbed to the rocking motion and the compartment fell quiet. Only the clatters and grinds of the bogie underneath could be heard.

For the purpose of making dialogue for this story, I visited the café car, but found it empty. I didn't want to be a sad, lonely man sitting there by myself, so returned to my cabin to be a sad and lonely man in private.

DAY 4:
NORTHERN SPAIN

I nodded off to sleep around midnight, and to my amazement, woke at 7am. I take being a light sleeper to a new level, so to discover I had slept for seven hours on a noisy, lurching train, made me lie down again in shock. The fear of missing the scenery outside encouraged me to get up again, take a shower (one of the few benefits of the Grande Clas cabin) and prepare myself for a long day of travel ahead.

The landscape of Northern Spain looked less arid than Portugal, with 50 shades of green. Trees and bushes looked more lush and lines of reaped wheat added to the palette of colours. I had also crossed my first time zone during the night, now one hour ahead of Portugal, and the first of many to be crossed.

I found Trenhotel reviews online, but most were out of date and often unhelpful. Many stated the train's decline, which was an accurate description. As mentioned, my Grande Clas compartment included a shower, and also a cheap amenity pack, and a 33ml bottle of water. The only interaction with staff involved the collection and eventual return of my ticket.

As we passed Miranda de Ebro, the Germans next door were stirring. I propped myself upright using two pillows, and watched northern Spain pass by. Overnight the land had gradually become greener, contrasting with the more earthy colours of southern and western Portugal, with my window framing the subtle changes to the landscape. This was what made train travel such an enjoyable experience. By Vitoria Gasteiz, the Germans were fully awake, and they began to fiddle with attachments and made jungle and howling noises whenever the train entered into the darkness of a tunnel.

We now entered a more hilly and forested region of northern Spain – the Basque Country. I studied my large, double-sided map of Spain, spread out on my sleeping berth. Whenever the train entered a tunnel, not having the reading light on, with my cabin plunged into darkness, reading a map became impossible. While in the dark, my finger remained positioned on the last landmark identified. At this point I wondered if Braille maps existed, and they do! They were called tactile maps.

The first clouds on this trip were spotted at Beasain. They looked as if there would be enough shade to prevent my British skin from being burnt to a crisp. Ferns and palm trees now complemented the view through the window. San Sebastian looked gorgeous in the morning sunshine as the light sparkled off the Urumea River and harbour.

Eventually the train arrived at Irun, the last station in Spain. This enjoyable overnight train trip would come to an end in ten minutes, once we crossed the Bidasoa River, and the border into France. I was disappointed, but at the same time happy to keep the momentum rolling on this journey.

I stood outside my compartment door to watch the passengers on the platform. The Germans were due to leave the train here. "This is Irun!" the conductress shouted in English to the closed cabin door. She knocked on the door several times. Father appeared, and dragged his oversized black bag along the corridor and out onto the platform, but his son didn't follow.

"Hurry, the train is about to leave!" she shouted along the corridor, standing by the carriage door to prevent the train's departure.

"You must come now! The train is now leaving!"

"I can't find my shoes!" shouted the boy. Our conductress rolled her eyes at me.

"You get off now or the train leaves." she warned. The boy scrambled out of the cabin, and dragged his backpack onto the platform, in his socks. She slowly shook her head, closed the door, and we bid farewell to the two Germans standing on the platform, son sans shoes.

The SNCF station at Hendaye offered no luggage storage facilities, although a helpful station assistant pointed me in the direction of the Café Ole across the road, so I walked over to see if they could help. A girl behind the counter was more than happy to look after my backpack for a fee, while I explored Hendaye. Most French stations don't offer luggage lockers, for security reasons, and the larger stations require all bags to be x-rayed.

The sign above the door of a nearby *pharmacie* indicated an air temperature of 24°C, but the high humidity caused my shirt to quickly stick to me. It always pleased me to see locals fanning their faces, which meant I wasn't just a lightweight traveller, unable to handle the local weather. What started as a cloudy day had become an overcast day, and as a result, an increasingly humid day.

The bridge across the Bidasoa River on Avenue d'Espagne marked the border between France and Spain. I love borders, a condition I call 'frontieraphilia' - a love of border crossings. A sign proudly listed all of Hendaye's twinned towns; Arguedas in Spain, Viana do Castelo in Portugal, and stopped in my tracks when I read the third town - Peebles in Scotland. Peebles? After a few moments I remembered Peebles was located close to the Scottish side of the border with England.

Hendaye's claim to fame happened in October 1940 when Francisco Franco of Spain and Adolf Hitler met at the station. Although Franco had cautiously aligned with Germany, he raised the request where Spain would gain Gibraltar and a number of other territories when Germany won the war. Hitler wanted to hold onto Gibraltar, since controlling the entrance to the Mediterranean Sea would be of major strategic importance. The fear of potentially showing favouritism towards Franco, and undermining Italy, a German ally, caused the negotiations to fail.

The TGV train for Paris left Hendaye exactly on time with my first class carriage almost empty. When booking this journey I stumbled across a special first class fare, at just EUR15.00 more than second class. Not a bad deal for a journey of six hours. At the first stop, Saint Jen de Luz Ciboure, holidaymakers scrambled on board to fill most of the empty seats.

I was joined, opposite, by an untalkative Frenchman in a pink shirt. Mr. Pink's hair had migrated from the top of his head to his incredibly bushy eyebrows. He began to read his Le Figaro newspaper, and gradually claimed each remaining millimetre of leg space not already occupied by me. Whenever he read anything interesting, his hairy eyebrows would twitch. Our toes were touching, although in fairness the lack of legroom facing first class passengers was surprisingly poor.

Once he finished reading his copy of Le Figaro, Mr. Pink slammed the paper down onto the table in a sort of 'I've finished' gesture. He then began to thumb his way through his copy of Le Point magazine, which was also slammed down when finished, and then began flicking through a book about research ships. When he first sat down, my gut instinct said he was perhaps a little strange. This 'I've finished reading' announcement of slamming down his reading material confirmed he was more than just a little odd.

By the time we left Biarritz almost every seat on board had been taken. At Dax a woman in her 40s did the usual stare-at-ticket and gawk-at-seat-numbers ritual. She walked along the carriage, and found her seat taken by another passenger. Ironically the occupant had already moved someone from that seat when he boarded at Biarritz. She showed the man her printed confirmation, he showed her his printed confirmation, and they did a side-by-side comparison. The woman looked puzzled, as if they shared the same seat number. I thought to myself, "This will be good".

I've had a fear of sitting in a wrong seat, or worse, someone claiming mine, for many years. A few years ago I boarded a flight, quickly found my window seat, firmly attached my seat belt, and ensured my seat was in the upright position and my table locked. Placed on my lap were a paperback and a packet of biscuits, ready for the journey ahead.

"You're sitting in my seat!" barked a rather annoyed woman standing in the aisle. My seat was actually one row back. Two passengers reluctantly moved from their seats while I vacated the window seat. I also had to shift a passenger wrongly sitting at my window seat, and also move those two adjacent passengers. This performance entertained an aircraft of staring passengers behind us, enjoying the pre-departure disruption.

It's not possible for two passengers to be allocated the same seat number, so I was keen to see how this problem would be resolved. The man wasn't prepared to move, so the confused woman walked to the end of the carriage where a car attendant stood, guarding the open door. After a lengthy conversation, she showed her printed ticket and seat reservation to the puzzled attendant. She then broke into an embarrassed smile, followed by laughter. She had either booked the wrong train, or my preferred stuff-up scenario, booked the wrong date. The attendant told her to stand by the door until he found an empty seat. While she waited, the confused woman indicated in gestures through the train door, to her friend on the platform, that there had been a cock-up. Her friend put her hand to the side of her head in disbelief as if to say "How bloody stupid of you." The embarrassed woman was escorted to another car, never to be seen again, and no doubt keeping a low profile.

Then an announcement was made through the train. Our departure from Dax would be delayed due to a problem with the power car at the front of the train. Passengers made a collective Gallic groan, and several stepped out onto the platform for a quick smoke. Mr. Pink slammed his book on research ships down onto the table in disgust.

Once the train eventually rolled out of Dax, I walked through to the café car for a spot of eavesdropping. There were four miserable-looking passengers standing alone at small tables, drinking coffee and gazing out of the windows. I decided to buy a bottle of Coke and a small brownie, and at the prices charged, I wasn't surprised the other passengers looked miserable as well.

While slouching over a standing table, trying to compose myself after the price shock, two train guards entered the café car. They looked at me briefly before approaching a young man who appeared to be a cross between a backpacker and a hippie. The train guards escorted him from the café car back to a 2nd class carriage where his 2nd class ticket entitled him to be – assuming he had a ticket, which may have been the problem.

A few drops of rain splatted against the windows, but the airspeed outside soon blasted them off again. Vineyards gave way to fields of grain, as we sped through the French countryside. TGV's on this route reach 320 kilometres per hour, which was rather swift, but not as swift as the trains I would experience in China.

We pulled into Paris Montparnasse station right on time at 8.30pm. Despite the seven hours of slumber on the Trenhotel, today had been a long day, which was now taking its toll. I had no reason to loiter, so caught the Metro Line 4 train to Gare du Nord, and walked to the Ibis

31

Paris Canal Saint-Martin. Within 45 minutes of arriving into Montparnasse station, I locked my bedroom door behind me, collapsed onto the bed, and immediately fell into a deep, non-rocking slumber.

DAY 5:
PARIS, FRANCE

I faced a full day of walking ahead of me, and knew some of the points of interest circled on my map would be missed, but decided to give it my best shot anyway. First on the map was the Parc des Buttes Chaumont, the fifth largest park in Paris. Cutting through the park lay the Chemin de fer de Petite Ceinture. These were the remains of a Parisian railway, which, from 1852, provided a circular train connection between the main Paris railway stations, similar to London's Circle Line and Moscow's number 5 Koltsevaya line. Passenger services ended in 1934 with the growth of the Metro, and complete closure in the 1970s when the demand for freight services dwindled. The tracks now sat abandoned, but by squeezing through a gap in a wire fence, I could scramble down onto the track bed, and walk along the line and into a cool, dark tunnel.

While wandering through the park, I passed a young woman practicing her yoga, shortly afterwards by a few women practicing Tai Chi, and two more moving in graceful slow motion performing a Chinese fan dance. Once outside the park I realised I had stumbled across a local Chinese community, and a taste of things to come further east.

Whenever I've visited Paris, the Sacre Coeur was a must-see, even though I've visited the basilica several times before. This pilgrimage was similar to seeing the Chrysler Building when in New York, riding the Underground when in London or visiting the Brandenburg Gate in Berlin. A tram trip to Glenelg when in Adelaide, and a visit to Kardinia Park in Geelong, home to the mighty Geelong Australian Rules football team, when in Melbourne, had to be done when the opportunities arose.

Walking up the curved path to the summit of the hill where the basilica stood, I noticed six African men ahead attempting to coax visitors into buying tourist tat. Their aggressive sales technique came as a surprise, when one grabbed me by the arm from behind. Making

33

physical contact with a potential customer is not the done thing. I hoped his sweaty experience had been as unpleasant as mine. At least the African leather goods sellers had been removed from the area in front of the Sacre Coeur, but they hadn't disappeared completely.

Wherever tourists walked, entrepreneurs could also be found. Cool bottles of water for sale were the hot item by the Eiffel Tower. Having just finished my umpteenth bottle of water, I fancied a bottle of chilled water sold from ice-filled buckets. I assumed these bottles would be filled with tap water and not mineral water, but considering I couldn't tell the difference anyway, what harm would there be? The fact it may have not been completely clean water didn't cross my mind, until later. A bottle cost EUR1.00, which matched the average cost for a 500ml bottle of water. When turning the blue plastic lid, I didn't hear the usual crack of a breaking security seal. The lid was tight to begin with, so the jury was out on this one. Wherever shade could be found, so could water sellers.

Dozens of Africans sold identical Eiffel Tower tat – various sizes of models, and metal keyrings. At The Trocadero, a popular Eiffel Tower viewpoint, opportunists were at it again. The majority of water sellers seemed to be Indian, and the tat sellers were African. The sheer number of men selling the same tourist tat suggested a case of supply seriously outstripping demand.

I wanted to ask one of the sellers if they had actually sold any items today. Suppose I wanted a cheap and tacky Eiffel Tower model, who would I buy it from? How would I choose between the dozen sellers all lined up? Would I base my purchase on the seller's smile or the way he had displayed the little brown towers on his blanket?

On the lawn in front of the Eiffel Tower, a few men weren't selling water, but from buckets they were selling chilled bottles of wine and even champagne. How romantic, but I noticed they weren't selling plastic glasses or cups. This value-added sales oversight was a missed opportunity for another Euro or two. I couldn't imagine classy, champagne drinkers in Paris guzzling straight from the bottle. How decadent.

In September 2018, French police seized 20 *tonnes* of miniature Eiffel Towers in an operation to dismantle an extensive network of

Africans selling illegal souvenirs and arrested nine men. Authorities continually struggle to control the counterfeit souvenirs sold by undocumented migrants. It was once leather goods. Now it's tourist tat.

I watched an operation near the Eiffel Tower. As a line of Africans sold their identical wares on blankets, a lookout stood on a street corner. As soon as a police officer approached, he signalled to his accomplices and they immediately grabbed all four corners of their blankets and slung their impromptu swag bag over a shoulder and bid a hasty retreat into nearby streets. The whole operation took ten seconds. They would no doubt return once the coast was clear.

I stumbled across a dodgy ball-in-the-cup game in progress, also called the shell game. As per usual there would be one aggressive gambler prepared to bet EUR50.00 per pop, throwing an ochre-coloured note onto the table without hesitation. This 'tourist' would be on a winning streak and the whole performance was loud and animated. An operator stood nearby wearing a bum bag (fanny pack), to hold the takings.

Even if the game was 100% legit, the odds were in the favour of the operator at 2:1. However, these games were never 100% kosher. Sleight of hand helped to improve the odds of the operator cashing in, and the pigeon cashing out. If you stand around too long, just watching, you will be invited to play along. One man approached me, and showing no interest in playing, I was told in French, I'm guessing, to bugger off.

Tourists were a funny bunch to look at. Here we had arguably the world's greatest icon bathed in the rays of the setting sun, and half of all visitors stared at their phone checking Facebook or Instagram. What's more important, the Eiffel Tower, or the latest photo of your friend's cat or dinner?

I finally arrived at the Arc de Triomphe at sunset, and paid a small fortune to climb up to the observation deck at the top. As expected, the corner nearest the Eiffel Tower was the busiest, so carefully nudged my way through the crowd to have a look. I found it amusing to see dozens of phones held above heads in an attempt to catch that magic photo, in a sort of 21st century homage to a 19th century structure. At any one time, at least a dozen visitors would be looking away from the view, taking photographs of their own faces with the Eiffel Tower in the background.

Here's an interesting fact. The Eiffel Tower light show began in 1985 and is still protected under France's copyright law as an artistic work. As a result, sharing or publishing photos of the tower at night without prior permission from the Société d'Exploitation de la Tour Eiffel was illegal. I wondered how many visitors broke French law unawares on a daily basis?

DAY 6:
PARIS – COLOGNE – BERLIN

Heavy rain slammed against my bedroom window, causing me to wake early. This first rain experienced on my journey was a reality check. So much for my dream of Portuguese sunshine following me all of the way to Vietnam.

In my day job I sold Thalys train journeys to corporate clients, but this would be my first time actually travelling on one. I was pleased to note standard class seats offered more leg space compared with first class on the TGV to Paris. Another rear-facing seat had been allocated which was unfortunate, as I prefer to see where I'm going, and not where I've been. Behind me sat two American women, first spotted at Gare du Nord station. They had enormous backsides and suitcases to match.

"He was pushing against me in the line. I felt like saying 'Fuck off and be more patient.'"

"Jesus Christ. I had the same happen to me."

"Why couldn't he be more patient?"

"I don't understand it. Jesus Christ."

"Remember the same thing happened at the line at the Louvre?"

"Yeah. If it's not jumping the line, it's pushing."

"Jesus Christ."

"Why do they always have to push?"

I struggled to keep up with the intellectual level of this conversation, so took a nap instead.

I woke near the Belgian border and found the rain had stopped. More importantly the two ladies behind me were now quiet. A sneaky look behind me, between the seats, revealed one girl updating her diary, and both, more importantly, were silent.

Fields had been recently harvested, dotted with regular, huge, round bales of yellow hay. Watching the landscape change outside your window was one of the many joys of train travel.

Across the aisle sat two rather large men. If you've ever seen

Ricky and Bubba on the TV show 'Storage Wars: Texas', then you'll get the picture. The American didn't say much, but the Danish man did, and his life sounded fascinating. He was bound for Cologne to attend the Games.com trade fair. He was a professional game tester, and regretted he had no say in the games he tested, although his favourites included a storyline. "The games where you just shoot guys get a bit boring" he said.

He had a young family, was well travelled, up-to-date with European news, and based himself in Brussels. He wanted to learn Flemish, and had recently travelled to Edinburgh, the home of Scotland's gaming industry. Rockstar North is based there, and if you've ever played some of the GTA/Grand Theft Auto games, you may have spotted some of the subtle references to Scotland. As a Scotsman, I find some of them hilarious, but most are probably lost on foreign users.

To my relief, the two loud girls behind me left the train at Liège. Why had fate chosen this great city to be punished in such a way? Jesus Christ. Let's hope no one pushes them.

At Cologne Hauptbahnhof I had to change trains, and with around an hour to kill, I took a quick look outside. People were sunning themselves on Bahnhofsvorplatz and on the steps leading up to the imposing Cologne Cathedral. Despite trying to occupy my mind, it took only 15 minutes for my resistance to break, succumbing to my first bratwurst. I'm only human after all. Each December I visit the Continental Market in Glasgow for the German sausages, and although always delicious, the genuine sounds of Cologne made today's bratwurst taste much, much better.

My next train was a high-speed ICE service bound for Berlin and I had been allocated an aisle seat (rear facing, naturally). The adjacent window seat remained vacant until Düsseldorf when a chirpy German girl named Anna joined me. She was in a flap as to what to do with her large suitcase, which wouldn't fit onto the overhead luggage racks. Solution: back-to-back seats provided storage areas between them, so I pointed this out to her. I had learned this trick earlier on this adventure, and it was an important one to remember if you wanted to be the carriage hero. Her girl friend stood on the platform and frantically waved goodbye. Anna did the same from her window seat. This mutual waving had continued for several minutes, when I decided to frantically wave to her friend as well, to see what would happen. This had the effect of animating the girl on the platform even more. As the train began to pull out of the station, Anna's crazy friend ran alongside the train window waving and jumping.

Anna was a student and heading for Berlin. She occupied herself primarily playing a type of Nintendo game, while she listened to music on her phone. She seemed keen not to talk to this crazy tourist.

A frail old lady also boarded at Düsseldorf. She took ages to find her seat, and almost as long to carefully fold up her coat and then throw it roughly up into the luggage rack above. I caught her eye, and she accepted my offer to lift her bag onto the luggage rack. The carriage hero had struck again.

BERLIN, GERMANY

I had visited Berlin a number of times, and can honestly say it was my favourite city in Europe. Berlin's population feels young, and there's energy in the air unlike anywhere else. I never tire of this great city, although it always leaves me feeling my age.

After check-in and a quick freshen-up at the Ibis Budget Hotel Alexanderplatz, the area of Berlin which was my regular haunt, I ventured out for a stroll. While shooting a photo of a yellow Berlin tram, a girl around 17 years of age, walked over, spoke to me in German, grabbed me by the arm and guided me in the direction of Alexanderplatz station across the road. For the record, this doesn't happen to me too often. Behind us walked four of her girl friends, wide eyed, laughing, and enjoying the confusion on my face. I read their facial expressions and they were thinking, "This will be good."

The gist of what she said, based on my limited knowledge of German, indicated that we walk over to McDonalds, and she should be treated to a meal, despite being a complete stranger. She was drunk, and the meal purchase wouldn't happen for a number of reasons. By the time I had regained my composure, and prised her hands off my arm, we had entered the station building. She was let down gently, and I waved an "Auf wiedersehen" to her disappointed friends. She didn't take long to find another man to latch onto. After this little bit of excitement, I realised I was hungry, but not for McDonalds.

I tend to be a creature of habit, dining at one particular restaurant, at least once, whenever visiting Berlin. Vincenzo's was a happy restaurant located right at the entrance to the Alexanderplatz U-Bahn station, and within earshot of the rumbling trains passing through Alexanderplatz station above. I recall, after a hot day of sightseeing a few years ago, I made myself comfortable at a table and ordered a large glass of Warsteiner beer. The glass delivered was a two litre glass, and being around 40cm tall, stood out like an amber beacon, warning all surrounding diners that a Brit with a drinking problem was in their presence. I hate being centre of attention. I put the size of the glass down to miscommunication. The kind waiter offered to pour the unfinished litre of beer into a bottle for me – a sort of 'doggy bag' for drinkers, but I declined. I know my limit.

Anyway, imagine my disappointment when I found there had been a change of management and also a change of menu. I decided not to eat there and checked out TripAdvisor later. Out of 251 reviews, 38% had listed the restaurant as 'terrible'. Oh dear. What had happened to my favourite Berlin eating place? For one thing, the restaurant had changed its name.

I walked along Grunerstrasse to a small German restaurant called Zum Paddenwirt, tucked away behind a lattice fence and a large tree by the Nikolaikirche. This lovely restaurant had been discovered during a previous visit to Berlin. Fortunately this hadn't changed hands and I could enjoy my meal of sliced pork tenderloin, followed by a bowl of Russian Solyanka. My Plan B restaurant in Berlin had now become my Plan A restaurant.

Solyanka is a thick, spicy and sour soup which gained popularity in the former East Germany by Soviet troops stationed there. I remembered, mid-meal, that the restaurant accepted only cash, so frantically fumbled around in all pockets, avoiding receipts, an old S-Bahn ticket and a paper clip, in search for enough Euros to pay the bill. I found barely enough to pay the bill, but no tip. My waiter took my handful of coins and gave a forced smile.

The plan of action was to walk back to my hotel, and not to be so inebriated I would need the assistance of the Polizei. I hiccuped, bid the staff a pleasant evening, and headed back in the general direction of my hotel, while fighting the temptation of a stopover at a bar for a nightcap.

DAY 7:
BERLIN, GERMANY

I feel comfortable in the Alexanderplatz area, knowing the whereabouts of a few restaurants, a couple of supermarkets and a large charity shop, for cheap emergency clothes. It's also a great place for public transport, whether U-Bahn, S-Bahn, tram, or airport buses. Alexanderplatz has it all. To be honest, I could live there.

Berlin has a couple of interesting markets and my favourite is Mauerpark. I caught the U-Bahn to Bernauer Strasse and walked the half kilometre to the entrance. With such a long distance still to travel, I hoped not to find any 'must have' bargains, otherwise they would be carried all of the way across Eastern Europe, Russia, Mongolia, China and Vietnam. It's still a great place to wander about and look.

Overnight rain had made the ground muddy. Huge, brown puddles had formed, which partially blocked the ground between the lines of stalls. Many stallholders looked less than happy, since visitors carefully stepped their way around these lakes, with hardly a fleeting glance at their stalls.

In a far corner of the market I found long benches piled high with assorted china, bowls and kitchen knick-knacks. This seemed to be a popular area of the market, so tiptoed around the puddles to investigate. On top of the benches sat dozens of old cardboard boxes full of assorted bits and pieces. I found several branded beer glasses and even more German steins. The idea of carrying them all the way to Ho Chi Minh City was a non-starter, but I made a mental note to come back one day with a fist full of Euros and a large shopping bag.

I had only one full day in Berlin, as tomorrow morning would see me leaving for Warsaw. I returned to Alexanderplatz to visit the Fernsehturm, 368 metres of East German concrete television tower. An orderly, lengthy line faced the counter to buy tickets for the observation deck. I have a love-hate relationship with technology, but with the clock ticking, standing in a long line for half an hour to buy tickets seemed a waste of precious time and worth the risk of interacting with a machine.

I took a deep breath and approached one of the self-service ticket machines. In 30 seconds I held, in my sweaty hand, my ticket and allotted time, only 15 minutes away. Perhaps the visitors in the line also had a techno-fear, not realising the multi-language ticket machines were the quickest option. I may have won against technology this time, but it would win the next battle. It always did.

My final task was to visit the town of Köpenick, 13 kilometres or 8 miles southeast of Berlin city centre. I love German football, and Köpenick is home to Bundesliga team Union Berlin. My plan of action was to make the pilgrimage to the town, have a look around, and visit Union's stadium. Their home ground had the attractive name 'Stadion An der Alten Försterei' (Stadium at the old forester's house) and was famous across Germany. In 2013, Union fans helped build a new stadium to increase capacity. Up to 10 professional builders worked at the site and 60-80 fans helped out. I couldn't imagine Manchester United fans building an extension to Old Trafford this way.

Union Berlin's football ground sat around one kilometre west of the town, and was easy to find along the busy Lindenstrasse. Approaching the main gate, my heart sank. Two men in hi-viz yellow jackets were ready to block my way. One man sat on a folding seat, and the other stood by his side smoking. I asked to enter the car park to take a photo, and held up my camera to help assist in the translation.

"Un momento." said the man sitting. He didn't look Spanish, and as far as I knew, neither did I. They exchanged a few comments and the first man replied "No." with a shrug of the shoulders, which indicated he couldn't give a toss whether I found this answer a disappointment or not. With Plan B in mind, I walked a short distance along the perimeter fence where a break in the trees allowed me to snap a photo of the stadium through the wire fence. I hadn't come all this way to Köpenick to be denied a photo.

All of this travelling stuff created a sweat, especially in the summer heat, so I returned to my hotel, freshened up, and hit Alexanderplatz for one last night in Germany, which unfortunately excluded a visit Vincenzo's restaurant.

DAY 8:
BERLIN-WARSAW

I watched the Warsaw-bound train leave Alexanderplatz station yesterday, and it appeared to be only half full. This morning I arrived looking forward to the journey to Warsaw, and found the platform covered by a layer of bags. Teenage students occupied the platform, most tapped on their phones, several just sat, a few crouched, and a few lay on top of the luggage mountain. Two slightly stressed teachers attempted to keep their students herded together in such a way to minimise inconvenience to other travellers. They failed.

Perhaps they were waiting for a later train, but as my train pulled into the station, 30-40 students began to stand up, find their luggage, and shuffle towards the doors. Still, things wouldn't be too bad, I told myself. Nope, wrong again. Our train wasn't made up of standard seating carriages, but made up of six-seater compartments, which was my least favourite type of train. Passengers were forced to sit face-to-face with strangers for hours, and battle for legroom. I could guarantee there would always be one passenger who would continually stare at me, and based on the expression it was never a sign of infatuation.

I found my compartment empty, but this changed moments later, when five of the students barged into the compartment, and took up residency. They were all animated, noisy and excited, with their Polish school excursion ahead of them. For me this would be a train travel nightmare. The students outnumbered me, and they took full advantage of the situation. They decided to spend the first 30 minutes photographing each other and pouts for the selfies as well.

A teacher appeared at the compartment door and handed the student their tickets. During their conversation 'Poznan' was mentioned twice, which meant the trip would be 3 hours of hell instead of 6½ hours. Don't get me wrong, kids are kids, but this would be nothing like a relaxing journey. They would continually stand up, sit down, stand up again and leave the compartment, with the door remaining open to reveal a crowd of grinning faces standing around in the corridor waiting to talk to their friends. I found it impossible to read. They leaned over each other, had a little play-fight, opened and closed the window and door, the curtain would be drawn, opened, and drawn again. I wondered which one I would kill first, as I was spoilt for choice.

My shins were accidentally kicked three times, I had my foot stepped on twice, and twice the aisle seat curtain to my left pulled shut, only to be opened again by me with the 'look of death' directed at the guilty kid involved. Maria was the best behaved and quietest of the lot, and described the compartment like a scene from a Harry Potter film. The boy opposite me may have been experiencing a testosterone rush due to the four girls in the compartment. He sat with his legs akimbo for the whole journey. More than once I thought about booting the target between them, to bring his cocky attitude down a peg or two, but decided against it, after balancing up the pros-and-cons. He came close when he took a short smoke from an e-cigarette after ensuring the door and windows were closed.

Fortunately for the boy opposite me, and his future generations, he and his friends did indeed leave the train at Poznan. A railway cleaner entered the compartment, and stopped in his tracks. He looked at the peanut shells, assorted wrappers, empty crisp packets, spilled bottles of drinks and signs of general mayhem. He looked at me with my shell-shocked face, and I just shrugged my shoulders.

Three men replaced the students. Opposite me sat a man in his early 20s complete with a face full of large, nasty pimples, and an equally nasty cold sore on his top lip. On a few occasions he mumbled to himself in Polish, but otherwise he remained quiet. The second man, also in his 20s, read a book called 'Futu.re', a science fiction novel by Dmitry Glukhovsky, and the third man, in his 40s, had a potbelly and fell asleep almost immediately.

At one point all three men dozed, which allowed me to watch a video on my tablet, and listen to music in peace. Outside, the flat landscape featured fields of wheat and corn below a grey and threatening sky. At one point a few spots of rain fell against the window, but the ground remained dry.

Leaving the Eurozone behind, each country from now would

45

have its own currency. I had also moved from a Germanic-speaking world to a Slavic one.

Fifteen minutes from Warsaw the men all woke at the same time as if aroused by an unconscious alarm clock. They quietly gazed out of the windows and looked in quiet contemplation of 'arriving home'.

My home for the next two nights would be the Novotel Warszawa Centrum. At the hotel reception desk, I decided to switch on the charm and ask for a high floor with a city view. Against all odds, it worked. Part of the evening was spent watching the lightning flash behind Warsaw's Palace of Culture & Science and impressive city skyline.

DAY 9:
WARSAW, POLAND

High on my list of visits, while in Warsaw, was the core exhibition at the POLIN Museum of the History of Polish Jews. I noticed the signage in the museum, at the Jewish Cemetery, and on the iron pavement markers, which marked where the ghetto wall once stood, were all in Polish and English. Poland's invasion by Germany in 1939 brought Britain into conflict, and ever since there has been a special relationship between the countries. Considering Germany shared an EU border with Poland, I found it surprising to see no German language signage. A Polish woman on a train later doubted anything 'anti-German' existed, saying English was the international language of travel. Also, Warsaw wasn't an important tourist destination for Germans. She might have been right – apart from one English/German restaurant menu, I saw no evidence of the German language, and heard no German accents during my stay.

I looked into this once I arrived home, and recent arrival statistics showed around one third of all foreign arrivals were actually from Germany, and German arrival numbers dwarfed the next largest market, Ukraine, by a factor of almost 3:1. I also checked a number of Warsaw restaurants online, and looked at their menus, and again, all were in Polish and English, but not German.

A small portion of the former Warsaw ghetto wall remained, but I couldn't find any signs pointing to this memorial. I stopped two locals, which on reflection, wasn't my finest moment. Imagine asking Muslim Turkish gents about the location of a Jewish memorial. They both spoke a little English and while one pointed to the back garden of a bland grey concrete apartment block, the other checked his phone for more information. A drunk staggered past, and hearing the conversation, asked me "Wall ghetto?"

I thanked the Turkish men for their help, and the drunk guided me to an adjacent street, through a nondescript gate and into the quiet, cool, shady courtyard of a four-storey apartment building. He claimed he needed money for food, but his ruddy complexion told me otherwise. I handed him 5 Zloty (around £1.00) and he seemed happy, although he probably made a habit of listening out for lost tourists. Either way, without his help this memorial may never have been found.

The air was hot and humid, with afternoon thunderstorms forecast. Satisfied with my ghetto wall visit, I watched the sky and managed to arrive back at the hotel just in time to miss a thunderstorm and torrential downpour.

'The Eye':- In suburban Berlin, in an area of tree-lined quiet streets and smart apartment blocks, I spotted a woman, standing between two parked cars, talking on her phone, and making no attempt to cross the road. She seemed happy just standing there, until she turned around, looked at me and said "Hallo". I nodded and kept walking, realising the nature of her business. Nearby stood another, much older, woman. She turned around and looked at me, as if she possessed a sixth sense. She held her glance, maybe just a little longer than usual between two strangers.

And then I saw a third woman, but this time her trade was blatantly obvious. She wore a bright orange short skirt and skimpy top. She spotted me and gave me eye contact. This all happened by a church, as the congregation began to walk down the steps and chat in small groups on the pavement. I didn't expect this type of trade in a leafy suburb of Berlin on a Sunday morning.

In Warsaw 'The Eye' was the same, but with a twist. The girls worked in pairs. One girl would give 'The Eye' and the other wouldn't be interested. Perhaps in Warsaw one girl conducted the business side of the transaction and the other acted as the minder or bodyguard.

DAY 10:
WARSAW, POLAND

Yesterday evening I asked the girl at the Novotel Centrum reception desk what time breakfast started, since my train to Warsaw departed at 7:50am. She told me breakfast became available from 6:30am, so at 6:31am I strolled into the restaurant to witness a food frenzy in progress. Over one hundred guests were already clearing the buffet counters with plates piled up high with food. One woman, sharing my table, bagged five bread rolls, and at the hot food table, after nudging me out of the way, a man slapped a generous serving of scrambled egg onto his plate, and several spicy sausages, four dumplings and bratwurst, the potato wedges, the mushrooms...

The quantity of food shovelled onto plates, the sense of urgency, and the sheer number of diners ensured breakfast wasn't as pleasurable as hoped. One of the highlights of staying in a hotel, which includes breakfast, is the breakfast. The spectacle bordered on gluttony on an industrial scale. It's not possible to relax and enjoy a breakfast when surrounded by diners pushing food into their mouths, while dozens jostled and nudged for position at the buffet counters.

Heavy rain woke me around 3am, and when I reluctantly checked out of the Novotel at 7am, the rain wasn't heavy, but persistent. I had loved my stay at the Novotel, and most impressed by the saxophone-playing duo in the bar last night. Maybe their renditions of the classics appealed to me, or the relaxed atmosphere, or perhaps it was the fact the two attractive female musicians wore short red dresses. I'm pretty sure it was the music.

By now the underground passages outside the hotel, where two busy roads met, were well sussed. I could now negotiate the labyrinth without finding myself diagonally across the intersection standing on the wrong corner. I had unknowingly become part of Warsaw's morning commuter crowd, and genuinely felt sad to be leaving this beautiful city and its warm, kind and helpful people.

WARSAW TO GRODNA, BELARUS

My 7:50am train to Grodna comprised of compartments capable of squeezing in eight passengers. This could have been a rather cosy journey, with a 5½ hour trip ahead of us, but we ended up with only six passengers in the compartment. By the time we reached Bialystok, where the train was divided into two sections, only the woman opposite me remained. She was a Belarusian national bound for Grodna on the Belarusian side of the border. No one in his or her right mind would voluntarily use this connecting service, via Grodna, to travel between Warsaw and Minsk. Direct trains operated between the two cities six days per week, and naturally today was the seventh day, so my only option was to connect through Grodna.

The train sat at Bialystok for 30 minutes, and the first Russian accents began to enter the train for the cross-border journey. Freight cars now featured the Cyrillic alphabet indicating how close we were to the border. Eventually the rain from Warsaw caught up with us, encouraging waiting friends and families standing on the platform, to retreat in the direction of the nearest shelters for protection. After some bumping and nudging, the Polish domestic carriages were removed from the train, a Belarussian locomotive was attached to the front of the two remaining coaches, and we trundled out of the station and in the direction of Belarus.

As the train rolled out of the town, a father and his daughter joined us. He was in his 60s and seemed to be struggling with a head cold. His daughter, named Anna Viktoria, looked late 20s. She was a beautiful woman, with blazing blue eyes, blonde hair, high cheekbones, subtle make-up and a little jewellery. She was mesmerising, and I studied her in great detail, but only after she closed her eyes for a nap.

A French violin player named Clara entered our compartment and made herself comfortable. She decided to finish her half-eaten kebab, filling the compartment with a kebab smell, which only kebab lovers would appreciate.

As we approached the Belarus border, the landscape began to

change.

Monotonous flat farmland, which spread to the horizon, and had dominated since the German border, now gave way to tree-lined hills, and the fields now appeared undulated and textured. Silver birch trees gave way to the Scots Pine, and I felt a sense of anticipation as we approached the border of Poland and Belarus, and the end of the comfort and protection the European Union provided.

The train stopped at Kuznica Bialostocka, which was as close to the border we could reach without crossing it. While we waited, I heard much movement on board, with passengers walking between carriages. As they passed our open door, hauling their bags behind them, these new arrivals couldn't resist a quick look into our compartment. The Belarusian woman opposite me changed her mobile sim card from a Polish to a Belarussian one.

A uniformed Polish officer arrived at our compartment door, and asked if anyone wanted a tax/VAT refund receipt. After a while, two uniformed men slowly walked the length of the train, glancing into each compartment. This was a warning to us all that officials were on board, and so no funny business would be tolerated.

After a few minutes a Polish Border Guard visited us. She took my passport and studied it for several moments before handing it back. Blue Belarus passports were checked and stamped with a Polish exit stamp. She requested my passport again, checked the photo page, and returned it to me again. She probably didn't see too many UK passport holders crossing the border at this point.

During all this activity, the rain caught up with us again, and down it poured in torrents. Right on time, at 12:34pm, the train lurched, and we continued on our way. I had entered country number seven, and my third time zone. Belarus changed to the Moscow Standard time zone in 2011.

The train rolled slowly forward, a little faster than walking pace, as if to add anticipation and excitement to the border crossing. On each side of the track lay a bitumen road behind which sat a high fence, light posts at 10-15 metre intervals and regular CCTV cameras pointing along the road and at the train. The cameras were designed to spot Belarussians accidentally jumping from the trains as they entered

51

Poland, without the necessary EU documentation. The border itself was anticlimactic, with a Polish red and white striped post standing next to a faded, red, white and green post of Belarus. A narrow clearance, carved out of the forest diagonally from the tracks, followed the invisible dotted line between the two countries.

On the Belarusian side of the border, a sole Alsatian stood in a small fenced enclosure, which included a kennel. The dog barked at the train, and its purpose was to highlight any illegal border crossings at this point on foot, although in what direction I wasn't too sure. Someone illegally leaving Belarus and heading for Poland would be seen as a problem for the EU, but would the Belarus Government really care less as this person disappeared, soon to be an EU problem? Their priority would be to stop illegal movement from Poland into Belarus. More importantly, why would anyone actually want to illegally enter Belarus, Europe's last dictatorship?

And then the fun began. After the passport check, an immigration officer stood at our compartment door and barked "Insurance document!" at me. I immediately felt a sinking feeling followed by an 'Oh Shit.' moment. My completed arrival card was handed to the officer while explaining the insurance papers may have been left behind at the Novotel in Warsaw. All eyes in the compartment were on me, and they were thinking, "This will be good."

The officer didn't seem too concerned and left the compartment. Unbeknown to me, I had been reported to Grodna security. We all stepped off the train, with our luggage, onto the platform at Grodna, and I shuffled with the rest of the passengers into the station building, as they knew the procedure. While standing in line to clear customs, I noticed the woman, who previously checked my passport, speaking to an officer. He wore a smart, brown uniform and a wide brimmed Russian-style military hat. They both stared in my direction, and I tried to tell myself they weren't watching me, but focussed on another passenger in the line behind me. After a few moments the uniformed official politely gestured to leave the line and come over to a small table. Remain cool, Manson. Remain cool.

A woman in her 30s walked over to me, and I soon discovered she spoke no English, but did speak a little German.With common ground established, she explained I needed to hold valid insurance. Proof of valid insurance was required when originally applying for my Belarussian visa, but unfortunately this piece of logic became lost in translation. Five Euros were handed over for a new insurance document, and she proceeded to complete the necessary form with agonising slowness. The clock ticked away, with 45 minutes before the departure of my train to Minsk. Remain cool, Manson. Remain cool. This was my first experience of Belorussian bureaucracy.

I felt this was just a revenue-raising exercise. Let's face it, if I had to make an insurance claim, how would I decipher a Cyrillic-language insurance document, obtain the necessary claim form, submit it, and what would I do with a cheque made out in Belarusian rubles?

With the insurance form duly completed, I joined the end of the now much shorter immigration line. "Insurance document?" asked the man behind the glass at the passport desk. I confidently slid my temporary insurance document over the counter to him, and breathed a sigh of relief when the unsmiling officer stamped my passport and immigration paper, and slid both back to me without a word.

As the 'Nothing to declare' green lane was closed, I reluctantly joined the end of a slow, shuffling line towards two customs officers, 30 minutes before departure of my train.

I preempted a communication problem by saying, "English only." and smiled at the unsmiling lady official. My biscuits, Snickers and a bag of damp clothing were all declared. "What is under?" she asked, pointing at another plastic bag. "Dry clothes" I replied, and the ploy worked. She gestured to pass, and within moments I found myself standing on the platform of Grodna station. With only seven minutes to spare, no time was wasted in finding the ninth train of my trip. The Cyrillic lettering and intimidating Soviet-style uniforms and officialdom all came as a shock, considering the ease of movement the European Union offered.

GRODNA TO MINSK, BELARUS

Seat 13 was in a berth compartment, and despite the unlucky number, I couldn't have been luckier. A woman occupied the seat opposite me. Two upper and two lower berths in the compartment could accommodate a maximum of four passengers, but it would only be the two of us all of the way to Minsk.

Russian pop music played throughout the train. Perhaps this noise was an attempt to generate a calm and relaxed atmosphere, similar to the music heard during the boarding process of an aircraft. After the trauma of the border formalities, I definitely felt more relaxed than before, but I knew the tinny music would eventually piss me off. Our train departed right on time at 3:12pm, the music stopped, and I was a happy man again.

I shared a compartment with a woman named Katarina. She was a Belorussian, but also an American, due to her marriage to a US citizen, and lived in Palo Alto, California. Katarina visited Grodna each year to see her grandmother, and would now spend four nights in Minsk before returning home. Katarina was a native of Grodna, and spoke Russian but she could also manage Polish. When I mentioned my knowledge of Palo Alto was better than average due to my corporate work, we spoke as if two long lost friends had been reunited.

It was a joy to talk with someone keen on languages, and to listen to her East European accent. "I still have trouble pronouncing words, such as the word 'beach' because that causes confusion." The word sounded like 'bitch'. After living in California for 15 years, the American accent was obvious, but the Russian accent was still there and a delight to listen to.

Katarina mentioned the Belorussian language was almost dead. I hinted this wasn't good for the national identity, especially when the Belorussian president couldn't speak a word. She lapsed into a silence and looked out of the window. Belarus president, Alexander Lukashenko, was regarded as Europe's last dictator, who didn't tolerate criticism in any way. Oops. That was worth remembering in future.

We spoke for hours. We discussed President Trump, California droughts, Belarussian beers, the various qualities of local salami, Brexit and how to pick wild mushrooms.

"Picking wild mushrooms is a Belarus tradition." said Katarina. "We call it a silent hunt."

"Can you preserve the mushrooms to eat later?" I asked.

"Yes, just put them into an airtight jar, and they will last over the winter. You can also freeze them. We also have hallucinogenic mushrooms, which look like toadstools. You get a sense of euphoria, but it can effect your sight and hearing."

"Have you ever tried these magic mushrooms?"

"No, but I know people who have. If you eat too many they might drive you crazy." Katarina circled her temple with her index finger. "You can buy preserved mushrooms in grocery stores too. Not the crazy mushrooms. The normal ones." We laughed.

I thought about buying a jar of mushrooms as a souvenir, but with many borders still to be crossed, and the customs formalities awaiting me, that idea was killed off immediately. Meeting Katarina would be amongst the highlights of this entire trip.

My home in Minsk for the next two nights would be the Hampton by Hilton, just a short walk from the station. I didn't fancy more problems on the Belarus-Russia border, due to the lack of insurance documents, so took advantage of the Hampton's 'Business Center'. After composing a short note, translating it through Google translate into Russian and printing it out, I showed the results to a member of staff at the front desk and asked if my note made sense. He said he understood the note. This was why I preferred English-speaking hotels – just in case of an emergency.

I needn't have worried though. Belarus and Russia form a 'Union State' where entry into one country guarantees entry into the other.

DAY 11:
MINSK, BELARUS

Friday seemed a popular day to get married in Minsk. Four newly wed couples were seen having their photos taken today. The brides looked stunning in their white dresses, and the men sharp in their suits. A photographer and a handful of bridesmaids followed each happy couple.

I wandered northwest from the city centre, along the bank of the Svislach River, to the impressively-named Belarusian State Museum of the History of the Great Patriotic War. The Russians and Belorussians don't refer to World War 2 as such, but to the Great Patriotic War, when the USSR defended the Motherland from Nazi invasion. Turning Eastern Europe into a protective belt of communist buffer states after the war tends not to be mentioned.

The realism of the human models in the dioramas came as a pleasant surprise. Too many museums displayed unrealistic dummies with shiny, plastic skin tones and unnatural poses. I stopped and studied the detail of these human figures, intrigued by the creases in their faces, shadows and authentic hair. These models left Madame Tussauds for dead. Even the grass looked real. The museum covers over 3,000 square metres and houses over 8,000 exhibits divided into 28 collections, showcased in ten themed halls. This was an impressive museum.

I was surprised at the small number of tourists in Minsk, with those strolling about dressed conservatively, looking like locals, and not a single example of SuperDry or North Face clothing anywhere. The city offered such a large selection of former Soviet architecture. Minsk was pretty much destroyed during World War 2 (sorry, Great Patriotic War), but the Soviet Union quickly rebuilt the city. Minsk almost became a UNESCO World Heritage site, but the application was soon put on hold when the Belarus Government realised this would result in a moratorium on any new property developments.

At sunset I caught the Metro to Borisov Tract station and wandered over to the seriously impressive National Library. This building design is officially described as 'a complex polyhedron of 18 squares and 8 triangles resting on a supporting podium (stylobate), with the surface covered by heat-reflecting mirror glass.' I couldn't have said it better myself.

Every evening, the building's LED façade becomes a free light show with over 4,500 light sources, producing over 20 light effect schemes with over 65,000 colours. I sat on a seat in a nearby park, which offered a fine view of the building. Unfortunately the mosquitoes ate me alive, but the spectacle was worth the biting. I hoped they all died of food poisoning.

DAY 12:
MINSK TO MOSCOW

I stood on the platform, by the door to our carriage, doing what the British do best – standing as part of an orderly, patient line. A smart, uniformed woman, known in Russian as a provodnitsa, guarded the entrance, and checked our tickets. In front of me two elderly ladies tried to board. One woman just managed to lift her wheeled bag from the ground level platform up onto the floor of the vestibule area. Belorussians don't use raised platforms, as we know them, but track level platforms resulting in a lift of around four feet.

The other bag, the woman said, was beyond her, and so the carriage hero offered to help. I barely managed to lift the bag up onto the vestibule, as it weighed an absolute ton. Our car attendant didn't lift a finger to help, perhaps held back by Belorussian Health & Safety regulations, although I doubt it. The other passengers waiting to board just stood there and laughed at my struggle.

Our train consisted of Russian-made rolling stock, made up of compartments of four berths. My cabin was already occupied by a Slavic man, slouched on the opposite lower berth. He wore red shorts and a black T-shirt, and until my arrival, had been dozing on his berth, filling the cabin with the stale smell of alcohol. This train began its journey at Brest, in the southwest corner of Belarus, where Sergey boarded. He'd had the cabin to himself, but that abruptly changed when I slid the compartment door wide open and grinned at him.

The foul cabin air was too much, so I threw my backpack onto my lower berth, and stood in the relative freshness of the corridor leaving the door ajar in an attempt to aid ventilation. A few minutes later the train lurched forward and we began to roll out of Minsk station.

Although just 9:30am, the car attendant offered me bedding, which confused me a little. Sergey, after a toilet visit, looked out of the window, took a gulp from a bottle of water and fell back to sleep. This suited me fine, as I now found relative peace, otherwise he would have scrutinised everything this crazy foreigner was doing – such as I was doing to him.

The cabin had a definite smell of piss. Whenever I sat down, the air forced from the seat beneath me released more of this unpleasant odour. The whole cabin reeked of urine and boozy breath.

We passed a small town, whose station's Cyrillic name passed by in a blur. Outside the beautiful, pink stucco station building, a smartly uniformed woman stood at attention on the platform, holding a small baton. Once the train passed by, she raised the baton to indicate all was in order with the train. We then passed two men riding in a buggy, pulled along by a beautiful golden horse; its white mane and tail flying behind as it trotted down a gravel road parallel to the tracks.

Sergey wasn't sleeping well. He kept tossing and turning, and letting out a disgruntled puff of air, similar to the hydraulic brakes of a train carriage.

Life outside the train began to look how I imagined European Russia would look; large chunky trucks, unrecognisable brands of older cars, men and women in rubber boots foraging for mushrooms in the woods, and babushkas in head scarves bent over and tending to vegetable plots.

Our train rolled through miles of pine trees, broken occasionally by the sight of mushroom pickers, standing in the middle of nowhere, watching our train roll by. Perhaps the noise of the passing train broke their 'silent hunt' concentration. At Borisov we passed freight trains, hauling coal, logs, woodchip, and natural gas. Sergey slept through Borisov, letting out a snore, having seen it all before.

By the side of the track, at regular intervals, sat small, white painted, concrete markers. These were 100 metre markers between kilometre posts, and dated back to the days of the USSR. The numbers were in descending order, marking the approaching distance to Moscow. From this point on these markers were difficult to ignore.

Not only could I see distance markers outside the train, I could also hear time markers inside the train. Sergey lay on his back, and at two-minute intervals he would yawn loudly, re-energising the rank smell in the cabin. At 11:15am Sergey surfaced again, ordered a coffee and two small cakes and made a phone call. At kilometre post 550, thirty minutes later, he rose again and poured himself a small vodka from a bottle discreetly hidden inside a blue plastic bag.

Our departure from Minsk had been under a cloudless blue sky, but now the sky had become a threatening slate grey. At Orsha, we stopped for a few minutes, and raindrops began to fall against our window. A man in an orange hi-viz jacket walked outside the length of the train, and tapped the carriage wheels with a small hammer. If the wheel rang like a bell, all was well. If the wheel was cracked, the sound would be dull, and this would be a problem for the whole train. This tapping routine was repeated at all scheduled stops.

Sergey fell back to sleep, pulling his white supplied sheet up around his neck. For him the journey became an opportunity to rest instead of staring out of the window.

We left Orsha, and the train continued its relentless passage through the forests. Occasionally a dismal, uncultivated and overgrown field would break the monotony of the trees, after which the scenery would return to more trees. Who owned these overgrown farms?

After the collapse of the Soviet Union in 1991, widespread cropland abandonment occurred, with Belarus hardest hit after 2000. Even today the Belarus agricultural sector remains largely unreformed, and is made up of collective farms, or kalhas (kolkhoz in Russian). Kalhas operated as state-owned enterprises, usually employing workers from nearby villages. In the days of the USSR, the kalhas was the centre of rural economy with almost all social life revolved around it. The Belarus leadership chose to preserve the former Soviet rural economy and community, which is completely unappealing to modern day Belarusians. Rural settlements offer a very poor infrastructure of culture and entertainment, and heavy drinking and fighting is not uncommon.

Farms offer very unattractive labour conditions. Occasionally workers don't get a day off, as they have to fill in for colleagues who are off work because they are drunk, or simply because of a lack of staff. Also, the Soviet-style management and contempt for initiative keeps young graduates and specialists away from kalhas. This encourages youth to move to the towns and cities looking for education, employment and entertainment. In fact many older workers also see better opportunities elsewhere, for example, in Russia.

Today, private farming makes up only around 2% of agricultural production, with the kahlas system continually subsidised. Alexander Lukashenko has been President of Belarus since 1994, and things began going pear-shaped in 2000, so this may just be a coincidence. There is little agricultural trade with the neighbouring EU, so avoiding a total collapse of the agricultural sector is dependent on Russia, who consumes around 80% of farming production. The country may have achieved independence in 1991 with the dissolution of the USSR, but has remained fully dependent on Mother Russia ever since.

There appear to be no up-to-date strategies to maximise agricultural output, and with the potential of a population revolt always around the corner, the only way Lukashenko can keep power is to keep a tight grip on the country and head an authoritarian government.

I guess that rant will ensure I'll never be granted a Belarus visa in future.

I walked the length of our carriage and discovered only two cabins were occupied - our cabin and the adjacent cabin where two elderly ladies sat, the same ladies I helped at Minsk.

According to my train timetable, Osinovka was the last station in Belarus before entering the Russian Federation. I felt a little anxious, due to the visa problems experienced when entering Belarus at Grodna, but also a little excited. It wasn't every day you had an opportunity to enter Russia by land.

Our train departed Osinovka, after a wait of a few minutes, and then rolled towards the border. Ruins sat in overgrown fields and the land could not have appeared more impoverished. There was no cultivation, industry, grazing or in fact any obvious use, only miles of monotonous trees and overgrown fields.

We rattled past a small, deserted, but modern platform. Who used this station? I guessed a farmer would drive miles to catch the train from this little station. Shortly afterwards I spotted small groups of mushroom hunters in a forest who seemed entirely focussed on their picking, and ignored our passing train.

Near Smolensk, farms became more numerous and more cultivated. A field of white goats passed by, with one goat standing on its rear legs, stretching to reach a leafy branch.

The train sat at Smolensk for an eternity, and eventually two other men joined us in our cabin. What had been, for hours, an almost empty train, now became a full train. Both new arrivals accepted their Russian Railways sheets and pillows, made up their upper berths, and lay there or slept for the duration of the journey to Moscow.

Imagine my disappointment when I realised we had entered Russia without seeing the border. We were subjected to no passport or immigration checks by unsmiling, intimidating uniformed officers when making the border crossing. Both nations formed a 'Union State', similar to the European Union Schengen agreement. Only when I noticed the change of car numberplates did it register we had entered the Russian Federation and my eighth country on this journey.

MOSCOW, RUSSIA

Despite on the move for ten hours, and the longest single train journey so far, this leg of the journey had been thoroughly enjoyable. However, the journey was over and I was excited to be in Moscow for the first time. Online reports stated the Moscow Metro could be a little daunting, but I impressed myself by understanding the ticket system and Metro route map without too much difficulty. Many of the Metro stations were stunning, and I could have spent many hours hopping from one station to the next marvelling at the Soviet influenced architecture. As trains roared into the stations at three-minute intervals, I made a mental note to try a spot of station-hopping tourism while in Moscow.

There were many Asian faces in Moscow, from Russia's Eastern and Southern regions. These were the first tangible signs of an approaching Orient, despite only 29% of the distance to Ho Chi Minh City having been completed. Moscow has a number of nicknames, some of which have a dig at the amount of new arrivals from the east and south of the Russian Federation. 'Nerezinovaya' comes from the saying 'Moscow is not rubber'. This refers to the fact the city can't continually stretch to accommodate all new arrivals. 'Poneekhalovsk' is derived from the Russian word 'ponayekhat', a rather rude verb used to describe the process of migration, and 'Moskvabad', which features the common suffix from Central Asia, no doubt poking fun at the large number of migrants from the former USSR.

My stay in Moscow would be at the Ibis Paveletskaya Hotel, a decision based not just on price, but location, being a short walk from Paveletskaya Metro station. This station was located on the brown Metro line 5, Moscow's Koltsevaya line, and linked most of the long distance railway stations. As line 5 was a circle line, getting lost would be difficult – even for me.

After a long day of travelling I felt tired, but also felt cocky with the Moscow Metro system. After sunset I caught the Metro to Komsomolskaya station. From here lay three terminal stations within a few minutes walk – Kazansky, Leningradsky and my destination Yaroslavsky. The Trans-Siberian Express was due to depart at 11:15pm, and hoped to experience the excitement and buzz of the boarding and departure of this great train. Imagine my disappointment when the train wasn't the beautiful, glossy, blue liveried train seen in travel websites, but the same bog-standard rolling stock used throughout Russia.

DAY 13:
MOSCOW

Before boarding tomorrow's train there were a few tasks, which needed completing. At the top of my list was the collection of tickets for the next two legs of my journey to Irkutsk and onto Ulaanbaatar. Now, I don't tend to mention names, unless they go over and beyond the call of duty, but *Real Russia* in London offered superb service. They answered my email questions quickly, arranged my Mongolian and Chinese visas, and also booked all trains between Moscow and Beijing. My train tickets were waiting for me at their Moscow office, and by handing over a piece of paper, the tickets would be handed back to me. The whole operation was quick and painless. So much for the feared Russian bureaucracy.

I also needed a haircut. With four nights of sleep on board a train without a shower, I feared the dreaded 'bed head' each morning, with hair sticking up in all directions. Such a sight would be very uncool and unbefitting a long distance train traveller. I found a barbershop, plucked up the courage and stepped inside. My middle-age barber who attended to me spoke a few words of English, whose vocabulary focused primarily on barbering terms. How fortunate, as I could have left his shop with a Russian military haircut, a trendy hair style or worse still a Spartak Moscow logo on the back of my head.

I returned to Yaroslavsky to see the arrival of the famous 'Rossiya' from Vladivostok. Again the train was compiled of less-than-impressive standard Russian Railways rolling stock, which lacked the glamour expected in connection with such a great train journey. This train could have been the 11am departure from Kostroma, and not a train, which had just completed a 7,621 kilometre journey from the Pacific Ocean.

Yaroslavskaya was one of nine main railway stations in Moscow, and boasted the highest passenger throughput of all of the capital's main-line termini. The station was named after the city of Yaroslavl, the first large city served by the line. However, the Trans-

64

Siberian line jutted off in an easterly direction before reaching there.

This stunning station building, opened in 1904, is described in architectural circles as 'Neorussian revival'. Around 300 pairs of trains serve this station, and the 'Rossiya' was one of them. I stood and watched the passengers disembark, rolling their noisy 4-wheeled suitcases along the platform and then remembered the long distance train traveller was expected to be on trains, and not just looking at them.

I watched a group of younger travellers, and thought how easy travel had become. My independent travelling began in the early 1980s, in an era of no internet, no Instagram, and no bi-lingual signs. I only had a well-loved and dog-eared Lonely Planet guide, and a determination to overcome hurdles as they presented themselves. Selfies hadn't been invented, although I recalled Japanese tourists in Sydney would bring small chalkboards along on their holidays. They would stand outside the Opera House, scribble the location and date on this board, and hold it to their chest while grinning at the camera.

In the early 1980s I couldn't keep friends and family up-to-date in regards to my whereabouts by posting a picture on Facebook or Instagram. Postcards would be sent in the hope they would arrive home before I did, or phone home from a public phone box, at an extortionate rate. Conversations would be short and quickly terminated because of a lack of local coins, and time differences also had to be considered, especially with my parents living in Sydney. Yes, today's travellers have all answers to all questions at their fingertips. So, when young travellers appeared to be in a pickle, fretting due to indecision, I had a strong desire to go over and give these poor, distressed travellers a good shake.

I taught myself to read Russian, although my spoken word was non-existent. Although bi-lingual signs can be found in Moscow due to the 2018 World Cup and the number of foreign visitors, reading the Cyrillic alphabet still had its use. Many Cyrillic letters look familiar, so my brain would try and convert letters into an English or a Latin equivalent, which would cause confusion. Take 'PECTOPAH' for example. That made no sense, but in Russian, the sign read 'Restoran' and now things started to make sense. I would never go hungry in the Russian Federation. Trying to read Russian was similar to a toddler learning to read for the first time. Russian shared around 24% of its words with English, although not exactly like-for-like.

Many major road street names included the word "Проспект". Imagine my joy, when the first time I stopped to read one such sign, it read 'Prospekt'. As I'd come across this word for such Russian streets before, this little discovery gave me confidence and a spring in my step. There would be no stopping me now.

All main stations in Moscow have security door frames, which passengers must step through, similar to those found at airports. Each piece of hand luggage must be placed onto the conveyor belt so a bored, uniformed officer can x-ray the item. If you're lucky a woman will scan you with a hand-held detector, otherwise, the process is uneventful. The purpose was to detect explosives although, to be honest, the whole operation appeared to be rather laid back. In fact, after 10pm, these security points were abandoned and unmanned. I mentioned this to a Russian man on board the train to Irkutsk and he said late at night would be the best time to let a bomb off, although the casualty numbers wouldn't be as high compared to rush hour. Adding to this sobering thought, he said "You could always hide overnight somewhere, until the morning rush-hour."

I wandered around and studied the dozens of brass statues at Ploshchad Revolutsii (Revolution Square) Metro station. Dogs were the most popular statues with commuters. A regular stream of passers-by would give the nose and paw a rub for good luck. Each statue in the station offered a certain type of good luck. Rub the female student's bronze shoe and this would bring luck in love and marriage, the flags held by a naval lookout resulted in having a good day, and the Mauser pistol held by a secret police officer would bring financial success. Another statue featured a well-rubbed rooster, which made me wonder what sort of luck rubbing a cock would attract? My initial thoughts were wrong. Rubbing the rooster resulted in financial gain, while others believed him to be an embodiment of evil things to come.

Anyway, after the necessary photos, I looked at the various statues and decided to give Ingus, the border guard dog's snout a rub and thought, "What's the worst that could happen?"

The tradition of rubbing statues dates from 1938, when engin-

66

eering students at Moscow's Bauman Technical University rubbed their report cards against the nose of Ingus, in the hope this would improve their exam results. This practice caught on with Muscovites and Ingus' nose now shines from decades of constant rubbing.

Within sixty seconds of rubbing Ingus, two rather attractive French girls walked up to me and one asked for help with a photo. This wasn't a strange request because when people see me holding a camera, they assume I can operate all varieties of photographic equipment. Did she want a photo by the dog? "No, over there. We like football." she said, pointing to another statue nearby. We walked over to a footballer statue, as I considered how much this moment had improved my Moscow street cred. We stood by the statue of a footballer with a ball by his feet. But wait! I had misunderstood their intentions. They didn't want me to photograph *them*, but the girl who first approached wanted her photo taken with *me*! My street cred shot through the roof.

I never did get to the bottom of this strange event, but after the girls left, I gave Ingus' nose another vigorous rub – just in case. On the same day four Russians stopped me on the street to ask for directions. This happens to me all of the time. Friends say I look approachable and look as if I know were I'm going, but four in one day was a personal best. After the French student requested my photo, I began to wonder whether people were mistaking me for a celebrity. After a few drinks and in poor light, covering up my good eye when looking in the mirror, I think I look like George Clooney on a really bad day.

The Moscow Transport Department has requested passengers to stop touching the statues, as years of rubbing the bronze figures left many of them worn down, losing their authentic look.

Before beginning this journey I had been training for my first ever half marathon. This exercise hadn't prepared me for long distance walking, which seemed to use different muscles. Today my legs ached, and I also managed to receive mild sunburn.

My legs screamed out when descending stairs, and I quickly came to realise how difficult less-abled travellers found the Moscow Metro. There are no elevators on the older Metro lines, and no shortage of steps. At one Metro station, a girl of 16 with cerebral palsy was carefully lifted from her wheelchair by her mother and older sister, and hoisted onto the first steps of the moving escalator. Meanwhile her father struggled with the collapsible wheelchair. With a helping hand on either side, the girl precariously descended the long escalator into the bowels of the earth. I gave the family a little space, and then followed them down to the platforms.

Moscow's Metro has a rule where travellers must stand on the right side of an escalator, similar to the rule on the London Underground. The trio in front of me (justifiably) blocked the full width of the escalator. From behind me came the clip clop of descending footsteps. I thought to myself, "This will be good". Sure enough, a woman in her mid-30s had her progress impeded and barked at the trio. I blurted out in English, despite the chances of her understanding me were slim, "You're not going to get very far. How about some patience?" The mother replied, in Russian, something a little more diplomatic. Mrs. Impatient smiled at me, which caught me off-guard, since Russians tend not to smile, especially to strangers. She apologised to us all in Russian.

15 seconds from the bottom of the escalator, the trio squeezed to the right to let this woman past. She probably wasted the saved 15 seconds on the platform waiting for the next train.

I dined at an open air Georgian restaurant. For a starter I chose the Batumian Khachapuri, a traditional cheese bread, similar to a small pizza with dough 'handles' with a fried egg on top. The main course was Pelmeni (pork filled dumplings). Starters normally arrive before the main course, but tonight I was half way through my Pelmeni when the Batumian Khachapuri arrived.

I always prefer local beers when possible. "Do you have Russian beer?" I asked the waitress while pointing at the beer list in the menu.

"Heineken?" she replied.

"Er, no. Could I have Erdinger?"

"That's not Russian" she said.

"Neither is Heineken. I'll have the German beer please."

Blankets, sponsored by Jim Beam, were draped over the back of each chair, and I thought nothing of it until later, when a number of female diners wrapped themselves in their blankets to protect themselves from the night chill. Considering how well Russians handle their gruelling winters, their inability to handle a midsummer night chill, as the temperature plummeted to +20° Celsius, came as a surprise.

While enjoying my magnificent meal, an orange moon rose from behind the silhouette of the Moscow skyline. If this wasn't stunning enough, the International Space Station moved across the dark sky, low on the horizon, skimming the rising moon. This glorious sight capped an unforgettable day.

DAY 14:
MOSCOW

Rush hour on the Moscow Metro was a learning experience. British commuters need their personal space, even in crowded situations, but not the Russians on the Moscow Metro. Pushing was necessary to board the train, while others pushed me from behind. Bumping up against each other was tolerated and carriages had no handgrips - in fact there was no need for them. I found myself wedged between strangers, nudging and swaying at each bump on the track. There was no need to say sorry when the train lurched, or give apologetic looks, when leaning on the person next to you. This was all part of the Moscow Metro rush hour experience.

I wanted a close-up look at Moscow City, which was Moscow's modern, high-rise business district. City bosses had the foresight and pride to preserve their city centre, by developing an out-of-town modern business centre. Paris has La Defence and London has Canary Wharf. London's city planners have permitted far too many eyesores to be built too close to the historic city centre – think The Shard, Heron Tower, 122 Leadenhall Street, 30 St. Mary Axe – you get the idea. Did these buildings have to be built adjacent to London's historic city centre, and also so tall? As Prince Charles once famously said – "Developers have done more damage to London than German bombers did during the war. You have to give this much to the Luftwaffe. When it knocked down our buildings, it didn't replace them with anything more offensive than rubble."

Controlled high-rise development doesn't just say commercial success, but hints at arrogance as well. Forests of glass and steel, in a concentrated area, contrast with the surrounding area, and says to everyone - "You can't help seeing our corporate muscle". Highrise development, in historic city centres, also hints at the need to make a buck over style or historic preservation, and this is a sad reflection on the attitude of some city bosses. Also, has anyone else noticed these phallic erections are mainly designed by men? I'm just saying.

I digress. Moscow City was a stunning, riverside collection of glass towers with unique and quirky designs. Thank God these weren't built next door to the Kremlin. Speaking of which, Red Square was filled with its usual quota of tourists shooting mandatory selfies. With the premium spot for the perfect photo shot found, and after carefully surveying the area, I extracted my camera and immediately two men decided to stand right in front of me. They both took a multitude of selfies, took photos of each other, all with the colourful St. Basil's looming in the background. I patiently stood there, watching them. They were oblivious to the person they just stood in front of, just six feet away, who was drilling holes in the back of their heads with his eyes.

Now it was selfie time with The Kremlin in the background. Oh hang on, we had better do St Basil's again. Did we do individual photos with The Kremlin in the background? I can't remember, so I had better do them again just to be sure. Hang on while I upload this onto Instagram. At times I have the patience of a saint.

GUM stands for Glavny Universalny Magazin ("Main Department Store"), and this iconic building was decked out in white lights and looked stunning. I stopped in a side street to take a photo. Just as the ideal position was found in my viewfinder, a young couple walked towards me. The girl saw me taking a photo, and as it was only natural for curiosity to get the better of her ("What's he photographing?"), she let out a squeal, whipped out her phone for a photo, while standing right in front of me. I swear she stood three feet in front of me, completely oblivious to the man behind her, with the patience of a saint, slowly shaking his head.

I enjoyed a captivating performance in Red Square. Four Indian visitors - three men and a woman in a blue, flowing sari – formed a small group. One man held an impressive movie camera, the second held a phone, and the third just stood there watching. Phone man pressed the app on his phone and music played, while the woman began to lip-sync and did rhythmic arm movements. This wasn't Bollywood, but the performance stopped me in my tracks. A small crowd joined me to watch this free, mesmerising entertainment. I wanted to clap and show my appreciation at the end, but I was busily packing my camera away when the music stopped. This was a good thing, as I would have been the only person clapping.

Russia has an appalling life expectancy for men, which is related to their lifestyles. Give a Russian man a motor bike, and he will ride as if racing in the Isle of Man Grand Prix. An open lane deserves full throttle, and with many of the main roads in Moscow having four lanes in each direction, this gave them the appearance of a racetrack when viewed through a tinted visor.

There had been recent protests against the Russian Government's aim to raise the retirement age. Putin's plan was to increase the age of retirement from 60 to 65 for men by 2028 and 55 to 63 for women by 2034. An estimated 40% of the male population won't reach retirement age. The World Bank estimated the average Russian male life expectancy was just 66, while the CIA's World Factbook said 65. Women could expect to live to about 77. This highlighted the average Russian male's lifestyle. Violence, smoking, alcohol and dangerous driving all added to this shocking statistic for men.

This also highlighted how wily Putin was. Imagine increasing the retirement age to that above the life expectancy. Think of the millions of rubles the Government will save in pension payouts. Russian politics is a fascinating subject, and leaves you relieved your local political system isn't as corrupt as Vladimir Putin's.

The 1993 constitution declares Russia to be a democratic, federative, law-based state with a republican form of government. However, Vladimir Putin believes otherwise, claiming Russia isn't quite ready for full democracy, and does all possible to reinforce this belief.

Occasionally, potentially successful candidates, standing against Putin's United Russia Party, find themselves arrested, or have their registrations withdrawn due to alleged invalid signatures or other minor infringements. The electoral system is known to discourage serious competition, transparency or accuracy, with regular reports of ballot stuffing. It's not uncommon for a candidate to be chosen, possibly with a financial incentive, to sit against a United Russia candidate. The bogus candidate has little chance of winning, but makes the ballot paper appear to be a democratically contested poll.

Occasionally opposition candidates do win regional seats, often with a local agenda, which is tolerated to give the impression of free elections. This 'non-systemic opposition' never has Kremlin approval, but helps the illusion of free and democratic elections. Should an opposition candidate become too popular, he or she will be brought down a peg or two, one way or the other.

I imagine in each regional office of Putin's United Russia, a number of staff are employed just to monitor and manage this version of Russian democracy. United Russia is formidable, and continues to have a chokehold on elected offices as long as Putin is alive and kicking. However, Putin was born in 1952, and with Russian male life expectancy around 65-66, you do the maths.

I guess that will be sufficient to ensure I never have a Russian visa granted in future.

I found Scotland's 'other national drink', Irn Bru, on sale in Moscow. For those not in the know, Irn Bru is an orange, carbonated drink with a strange flavor, which is a closely guarded secret. Scottish-Russian relations seemed to be at a healthy level. This observation was not to go unrecorded, so with Facebook in mind, I shot a selfie in front of St. Basil's, while holding a bottle of Irn Bru. It's a Scottish thing. In the meantime, tourists, with the patience of saints, stood out of view waiting for me to hurry up and move out of their viewfinders.

There is a belief in Scotland we are the only country in the world where a local drink outsells Coca Cola. Imagine my disappointment, when I learned this was an urban myth. Joining Scotland are such countries as Peru (Inca Cola), Saudia Arabia and the Middle East (Vimto) and Cuba (TuKola).

High up on Tripadvisor's 'must do' list was a visit to Izmailovsky market. I reminded myself not to buy anything as the idea of carrying purchases all of the way to Ho Chi Minh City didn't appeal to me. 84% of Tripadvisor feedback described the market as 'very good' or 'excellent'. To save time, I did a little pre-departure research on how to find the place. Yet again, Google Maps' accuracy was a little hit-and-miss. It suggested catching the Metro to a nearby station and hike a few kilometres. Based on my track record with Google Maps, I should have anticipated a problem. I discovered a Metro station right at the site, which didn't show on Google Maps.

Izmailovsky market, at first glance, looked like a cross between a market place and Disneyland. Once inside, the architecture was compelling, with pseudo-Bavarian wooden chalets, and many shops displaying no obvious retail purpose.

Most of the shops were securely shut, and those open for business only sold tourist tat – Russian Dolls of many themes, the most recognisable face being that of Vladimir Putin, Russian hats of all colours and amber jewellery. Dozens of stalls all sold the same merchandise, one after another after another. Surely this retail overkill couldn't be profitable? I found the same situation in Paris with the Africans selling identical Parisian tourist tat. Perhaps the full capitalist spirit had yet to filter down to all entrepreneurs. Diversify and succeed? One stall displayed old cameras and another sold LP's, both busy with customers. Russian doll stalls had no customers at all, and the owners all looked bored, staring at their phones.

I'm happy to report the only elevator I used in Moscow was inside my modern Ibis Hotel. There are an estimated 120,000 elevators in Moscow, over twice as many as New York City. Many are old, with 25% in the Russian capital having exceeded their lifespan. It's not uncommon to be trapped in a Moscow elevator. Elevator entrapment experts believe the numbers range between 120,000 and 200,000 per year. In comparison, Chicago, which has under a quarter of the number of lifts as Moscow, has the number of annual entrapment incidents reported closer to a hundred. The moral of the story is, when in Moscow, use the stairs.

I needed to buy supplies for my train journey – sausage, cheese, beer, bottles of drinking water and smaller assorted snacks. Russians had no need for canned fruit as shops had plentiful supplies of fresh fruit, so the idea of preserved fruit in a can appeared to be bizarre in this country. My heart was set on tucking into a large can of fruit salad, as the Siberian countryside passed by my train window. Eventually I found a shop, which sold canned fruit, but it was like finding a needle in a haystack.

I wanted to absorb the atmosphere of Yaroslavsky station, prior to my big journey, so arrived two hours early. After all, how many times would I board the Trans-Mongolian at Moscow? While watching the train departure board, an old woman laden with bulging holdalls approached me. She started speaking to me in Russian, and the gist of her question was why the train to Abakan wasn't showing a platform number on the departure board. I suggested, in my best English, that I didn't have a clue, but how nice it was to talk to her all the same. After a few minutes the Abakan train was shunted alongside platform 3. She joined several hundred other waiting passengers, and shuffled her way to the train.

Train 002, called 'Rossiya' was due to depart at 11:45pm, unlike my drab, unnamed, numbered 'train 004' which left 10 minutes later. My train would take 30 minutes longer to reach Irkutsk, but on a journey of 74 hours, an extra 30 minutes on this famous route was a bonus. Unlike the famous 'Rossiya', my train was primarily made up of Chinese carriages, and was also a fraction of the price.

My seat reservation was berth 17, carriage 3, located at the very rear of the train. Bedding was included in the price, and included a towel. I brought a towel along just in case, since online reports are often a little hit-and-miss when it comes to accuracy.

My travelling companions included a Russian woman in her early forties, and her son Alex. She occupied the lower berth opposite me, and Alex claimed the upper berth. On the upper berth above me lay a woman in her forties. Rear facing seats had been the norm on this trip, so imagine my surprise, and relief, when I found I was facing forward for the next four days. Our carriage corridor was on the right (south facing) side, which meant we would be on the shady side of the train. As Russian trains run on the right hand track, we would always see the constant blur of passing freight trains to our left.

There are things that can't be avoided, so thirty minutes out of Moscow I visited the toilet. At this early stage the toilet already stunk, and unlike Russian Railway's modern trains, this older one allowed the toilet waste to plop right onto the tracks. Toilet paper was provided, which was another online inaccuracy. I brought my own roll with me just in case, which would come in very handy later.

DAY 15:
SOMEWHERE WEST OF THE URALS

I didn't sleep well, unlike on the train from Lisbon to Hendaye, when I slept like a log. We reached Vladimir on time at 2:58am, where the train sat for exactly 26 minutes. In the quiet of the compartment, the woman opposite and the woman above both snored away, and Alex breathed heavily. I pulled the curtain open a few inches, and saw a totally deserted platform.

I was semi-conscious as we pulled into Nizhny Novgorod, with it's colourful apartment buildings, bathed in early morning sunlight, dead on time at 5:48am. Everyone else in the compartment was still asleep. Nizhny Novgorod received a good write-up online and I now regretted not having a stopover here, and instead pass straight through. Maybe next time.

Although drowsy, I wanted to be awake when we crossed the mighty Volga River. Approaching the Borsky Bridge, the line curved to the left, and peering through the window I could see the train ahead curving away. A Russian red and grey locomotive pulled us along, with a line of bland, green, Chinese carriages trailing behind.

In fact the train was almost entirely Chinese. Russian domestic passengers were allocated the Russian carriages at the rear of the train, which would be uncoupled at Irkutsk, and the Mongolian and Chinese-bound passengers placed in the Chinese cars. This made sense. I wondered whether walking the entire length of the train was possible, and see the Chinese carriages first hand. There was only one way to find out.

The Trans-Siberian and Trans-Mongolian routes were popular among foreign backpackers and a practical part of life for many Russians. Having a foreigner share their cabin had a certain amount of novelty value. Also, on Russian trains, as no gender separation in sleeping compartments existed, the beginning of each journey had an element of excitement and surprise. Sharing a cabin was like a lucky dip. Sometimes you scored someone worthwhile, and sometimes you bombed out.

Borsky Bridge, over the Volga River, was built in 1935 and reached an impressive 1,608 metres in length. In the morning light the silver truss bridge looked imposing. The river appeared very narrow for such a long bridge. Much of the structure carried the tracks over the floodplain on the far side of the river. With the Volga River seen, I lay down and drifted into an uneasy slumber.

I woke with a start at 9:30am. Mother, on the opposite side of the compartment, was already dressed and reading. Alex and the woman above me were both still fast asleep. I made a cup of tea and ate my Klasseyaeskeey cheese and smoked sausage for breakfast while watching the passing landscape. I was a happy man, and very fortunate to be travelling across Russia on this famous train.

My expectation of Russia was to pass through countless miles of primeval forest. There were trees on each side of the track, but gaps in this narrow 'green belt' occasionally revealed ploughed fields in the background. I wondered if these trees were planted by the tracks as a visual barrier to hide the fields beyond from the prying eyes of train passengers back in Soviet times.

We passed small towns centred around lumber yards. Harvesters picked up logs and placed them into neat piles. We passed rakes of multi-coloured oil tankers, a few clean, but most filthy with spilled black oil. Railway workers in orange Hi-Vis jackets strimmed trackside grass, and amongst the trees sat dark, wooden houses, with their own large vegetable gardens. Mother wasn't interested in rural Russia, as she had seen it before. She focussed her attention on her phone because where you had civilization, you had Wi-Fi reception.

We passed through Kotel'nich, known in palaeontological circles as a hot spot for Pareiasaurus fossils. Let's face it. I'm sure most people, at some point, have wondered where they came from. These 3 metre long reptiles called Europe, Asia and South Africa home 250-260 million years ago. This was the only claim to fame this town enjoyed, although I was pleased to note Kotel'nich appeared on the other side of a crease where I folded my Russia map. Good progress was being made.

We arrived at Kirov, right on time at 12:09pm, 917 kilometres from Moscow. This would be the last station in the GMT+3 time zone.

Kirov marked the ⅓ point of my End-to-End journey. I stepped out onto a platform for the first time since leaving Moscow, for a little fresh air, and to stretch my legs, conscious of not wandering too far. Passengers often had little notice of the train's imminent departure. One website (https://waytorussia.net) warned: "The trains along Trans-Siberian stop only for 5 to 20 minutes. If you decide to go outside, be careful: you may hear the hiss and the train might start leaving. They say they don't wait for the passengers. In case you're late for the train, you have two options: either go to the station's master and ask him to contact the train to get your stuff off the train at the next station (and then you take another train to reach the next station yourself). Another option is to quickly run for a taxi and get them to follow the train till the next stop." Either way, standing on the platform with your mouth open, watching the train depart, would be rather inconvenient.

To offer such a detailed description on this scenario, I felt this must happen on a regular basis. In Paul Theroux's 'The Great Railway Bazaar' he wrote about a passenger named Richard Duffill, who stepped out from his carriage at Domodossola and missed his train when it departed. His surname became a verb in this novel – to be Duffilled. As I didn't wish to be Duffilled in deepest, darkest Russia, one eye was kept on the platform, one eye on the stationary train, and an ear open for the hiss of air brakes.

I still had supplies bought in Moscow, so had no need to purchase anything from the platform shops. Shop vendors shared the same appearance - short, curvy, unsmiling women all wearing headscarves. In Russia it was important to know the difference between a babushka and a babushka, to avoid any accidental insult to the ladies on the platform. A BAHbooshka is an old Russian woman or grandmother, and a baBOOSHka is a scarf worn on the head by a woman or girl and tied under the chin. Confusingly, BAHbooshkas often wear baBOOSHkas. A friend of British singer Kate Bush once had a cat called Babooshka. She also heard the word used on TV and read the word in a magazine. Her single released in 1980, called 'Babooshka', would become her most successful worldwide hit, and to think it was named after an old woman or her headscarf.

Suddenly a station announcement was made, and immediately

78

Marina, the provodnitsa, began to call us all on board. This clue highlighted the train's imminent departure, but with so many announcements made at Russian railway stations, unless the language was understood, one announcement was as unhelpful as the next. Always keep an eye on your provodnitsa.

After departing Kirov we passed a Kvass brewery. Kvass is a slightly alcoholic brew, made from fermented rye bread. It was an acquired taste and I had insufficient time in Moscow for the taste to become acquired. Rye bread wouldn't be my first choice of bread and Kvass wouldn't be the worst drink I had ever consumed, but neither was it the best. Kvass reminded me of rye bread flavoured Coca-Cola.

I walked the length of our carriage, and discreetly peered into each compartment. We had at least four children in our carriage, and fortunately no loud, sweaty Russian men, drunk on vodka, which had been a lingering fear of this train. I was also the only foreigner in this carriage. While passing Marina's small cabin I had a sneaky peek to see how a provodnitsa lived. Marina was the day attendant, Natalya the night attendant and I got the impression neither would tolerate any nonsense from a crazy foreign tourist, or anyone else for that matter.

Freight trains passed by the left side of our train at seven-minute intervals, made up of around 50 wagons each. Behind the wagons were rotting huts surrounded by overgrown fields. We passed Yar, dominated by huge piles of thin logs sitting by the trackside, and oil and coal hoppers occupying most of the adjacent tracks.

It was near Yar when I noticed, or more accurately paid attention to, my first Russian level crossing. Not only do level crossings include the red and white boom gates, which are designed to discourage drivers from colliding with passing 50-wagon oil trains, but the roads also housed massive steel plates, which lifted out of the road surface at the same time. On the off chance our Russian driver was a little impatient and decided to skirt around the boom gate, his car would come off second best against this solid crash barrier. These types of barriers can be found at airport checkpoints, where they are called airport high security Hostile Vehicle Mitigation road blockers, or thankfully, abbreviated to HMVs.

Our train sped through the station at Glazov, which was a

shame. This town has a nickname – Glasgo, after my very own Glasgow.

We arrived at Balezino on time and we sat there for 26 minutes, which gave passengers plenty of time to walk along the platform and overhead pedestrian bridge linking the platforms. While at the station, the train would undergo any required maintenance; wheels would be tapped with a hammer to check their integrity, and the locomotive would be changed from an AC to a DC one. I bought a small loaf of white bread for 40 rubles and a tub of ice cream for 30 rubles. Marina stood on the platform, by the carriage door, watching over her passengers. She was a short, rather heavy, unsmiling battle-axe with short hair. Her face suggested she had survived (and won) hundreds of passenger disputes.

I thought about the miles these provodnitsas must chalk up while on the job, and how they ranked with other professions. The crew of the International Space Station would cover the most miles. Next would be the cabin crew from long haul air routes, followed by our provodnitsas, which was quite an achievement. Next would be the crew on container ships.

A train, comprised of natural gas tankers, rumbled through the station, breaking the relative tranquillity. Sure enough, the train contained fifty wagons. Many were light blue, others green, some off-white, and a few completely filthy, making it difficult to tell the original colour. As half of Russia sits on oil basins, it was impossible to speculate where these tankers had begun their journey.

Alex caught my eye as I wandered along the platform. Unfortunately due to his limited English, our conversation went like this:

"Where are you from?" he asked.

"Glasgow, Scotland."

"United Kingdom?"

"That's right. Where are you travelling to?" I asked.

"Zima" he said, and turned his attention to his phone. End of conversation.

Considering the tension between Russian and the UK in recent years, due to the occasional Novichok poisoning, he perhaps thought best to keep his distance. There wasn't much conversation between us for the rest of the journey. Alex looked in his mid-twenties, tall, thin, with shoulder-length hair, and I decided he was a bit of a mummy's boy.

After the train rolled out of Balezino, I took a short nap, having not slept well last night. I woke after an hour and opened one eye to survey my surroundings. Alex was reclining on the lower berth, while his mother squeezed his facial pimples and picked his facial scabs. I began to wonder whether 'mother' was perhaps not a mother at all, but someone a little closer. Perhaps she just looked older, a lot older, but this idea vanished when Alex called her 'mama', and he sat up and positioned himself close to her. They were an odd couple.

In 1830, a peasant near Perm killed his child as an offering for sin and buried the body in an anthill. This appears to have been a one-off event, and fortunately not a regular activity, but unfortunately Perm had since become famous for another person. From 1940 to 1957 the city was named Molotov in honour of Vyacheslav Molotov. He was a Soviet politician and diplomat, an Old Bolshevik, and a leading figure in the Soviet Government from the 1920s, when he rose to power as a protégé of Joseph Stalin. He did not invent the 'Molotov Cocktail'; the crude incendiary device made from a bottle filled with flammable liquid and a means of ignition. Unfortunately for Molotov, he is now remembered for having this weapon named after him, and not much else.

Finns coined the name "Molotov cocktail" during the Winter War as an insulting reference to Vyacheslav Molotov, who was one of the architects of the Molotov–Ribbentrop Pact signed in late August 1939. The Finns widely mocked the pact with Nazi Germany as was much of the propaganda Molotov produced to accompany the pact. This included his declaration on Soviet State radio that bombing missions over Finland were actually airborne humanitarian food deliveries for their starving neighbours. Finns sarcastically dubbed the Soviet cluster bombs "Molotov bread baskets'. When the hand-held bottle firebomb was developed to attack Soviet tanks, the Finns called it the 'Molotov cocktail', as 'a drink to go with the food'.

Perm was an important railway junction on the Trans-Siberian Railway from where lines radiated to Central Russia and the northern region of the Urals. The pride and joy of Perm was the zoo where rare snow leopards and Amur tigers could be found. The city also had a walking bear, or at least a bronze sculpture of one, the symbol of Perm. Locals believed, if the bear's nose was rubbed, this would bring good fortune, which I assumed would be better than the unfortunate snow leopards and Amur tigers who lived their lives behind bars in the Perm zoo.

Perm introduced itself with huge marshalling yards full of hundreds of grey, black, green and yellow oil tankers. This may have been a colourful sight, but also portrayed a sense of industrial grit. Perm's skyline loomed in the background, and at first didn't appear to be an attractive city. The Kama River flowed through Perm, so I stood in the corridor to watch the crossing, joined after a few moments by a number of adults and children for the same reason.

The stop at Perm was scheduled to be 20 minutes, so I climbed down the steps and took a quick exploratory walk along the platform to see how far along I would find the restaurant car. It was the adjacent car. In fact, we only had two Russian carriages on this train, and one was a restaurant car.

I had been napping until Marina arrived to vacuum our compartment floor. Marina had a number of daily domestic duties to be carried out. After the vacuuming, she swept the corridor floor, followed by a comprehensive mopping. Marina took a great deal of pride in the cleanliness of her carriage and the welfare of her passengers. She would check the toilets every hour to ensure they were spick and span – and they always were.

I stood in the corridor, staring out of the window, when we passed a small, white concrete post number 1403 on the right hand side of the track – 1403 kilometres from Moscow. Did you know there are around 2,640 concrete railway sleepers per kilometre of track? Neither did I until I read an article about the hypnotic effect of staring at passing railway tracks for too long. During one such trance I noticed the parallel track, which I had been focussing on for too long, started to gradually pull away from our line, and branched away towards an ugly power station. Behind the trees were dozens of coal hoppers, assorted concrete eyesores, a tall storage silo and a type of conveyor belt contraption. Just when you start to fall in love with Russia's natural beauty, there would be an ugly blot on the landscape, as a subtle reminder not to get carried away.

I also noticed an increase in noise from compartment number 4 next door. They were having a great time, laughing and occasionally spilling out into the corridor, and definitely more fun than the pimple-squeezing duo I had to face.

The sky had turned an ugly grey, to match the ugly grey landscape.

Drops of rain splattered against the windows, but we appeared to have missed the worst of the showers. A black Toyota Hilux bounced its way through brown puddles on a rough track. Nearby sat dirty greenhouses, dark, damp wooden houses, vegetable gardens and ruins. Within a few minutes we passed completely dry roads, but the houses were just as dismal as before.

In Moscow, while buying supplied for my train, I also stocked up on a couple of beers. As the drinking of alcohol wasn't permitted in the train compartments, I discreetly poured my can of German Paulaner into a blue plastic mug. As it turned out, I needn't have worried, as this rule was generally ignored. As long as you don't get too boisterous, the provodnitsas turn a blind eye. I convinced myself a little drink would help me sleep, although a reason to drink German beer wasn't usually required.

My stealth-like consumption of alcohol can be traced back to the mid-1980s. A friend invited me to a cricket match at Sydney's SCG, to which I reluctantly agreed. We spent several hours of boredom sitting on 'The Hill', a grassy observation area now consigned to the cricketing history books. During those hours, while I worked on my suntan and swatted flies, I noticed many cricket fans had brought oranges to the match, and the crowd was gradually becoming more and more animated. I learned these fans had injected vodka into the oranges, and brought the fruit into the ground as a way of circumventing strict alcohol rules. Needless to say, I was most impressed, and this Aussie ingenuity has stayed with me all my life. It also says something about cricket when you have to be drunk to have a good time.

DAY 16:
ASIAN RUSSIA

During the night we passed from Europe to Asia over the Ural Mountains. Our train lurched to the left, to the right, and back again for hours on end. The rough ride ruined any of the benefits from my Paulaner nightcap. We passed a white obelisk at the 1777 kilometre point, which marked the continental divide. This memorial features a Soviet-era globe and an orbiting spaceship. Unfortunately we passed this spot in the dark of night.

In the very early morning we rolled out of agricultural Russia, through dense deciduous forests, and eventually into Yekaterinburg. The city was known as the 'window of Asia' and for being slap-bang in the middle of the Eurasian continent. For me the city acted as a gateway to Siberia.

Yekaterinburg had a circus building, and prided itself in having, possibly, the tallest incomplete architectural structure in the world, the Yekaterinburg TV Tower. This was a title where I imagined there would be few serious competitors. The only other unfinished tower I could think of was the Montreal Tower, uncompleted after the 1976 Summer Olympics. The city also had a number of unusual monuments, such as a monument dedicated to Michael Jackson, despite him having never visited the city, and a curious keyboard monument. For people into keyboards, this artwork represented a QWERTY/JCUKEN IBM PC compatible Cyrillic computer keyboard at 30:1 scale. As a person who uses a keyboard daily, this would be a Land of the Giants inspired nightmare for me.

I peeked behind my curtain window and found an empty platform. We left around 3:52am, and I fell back to sleep, waking up again as we approached Tyumen. The sun belted through the window, so a quick refreshing wash would wake me up. Unfortunately Marina had locked the toilet, and it would remain locked until well out of Tyumen. I felt sticky, nasty and well, to be honest, needed a pee.

Our carriage lost a few passengers at Yekaterinburg and gained a few new faces in return. Overnight the view had changed dramatically to a completely flat landscape, one almost bare of trees.

I brought along with me a printed timetable of the train journey, but the times didn't correspond with the times on the corridor timetable. Train arrival times varied by an hour or two. I brought a detailed map with me, so always knew where I was - I just didn't know **when** I was. We were now in a new time zone two hours ahead of Moscow. My watch said late morning, but my stomach told me early morning. My stomach was beginning to fall out of sync with my brain.

In 2018 Russian Railways changed their timetables from displaying Moscow time, to displaying local time. The Soviet Union introduced the Moscow time rule to achieve consistency across the network. Passengers were no longer subjected to the inconvenience of continually changing their watches, which on reflection, would have been the least of their worries living in the USSR. However, this system continued to cause much confusion, especially with travellers in the post-Soviet era.

In 2018 I bought a local train ticket through the Russia Railways website, not realising the time change had taken place, and ended up buying a (fortunately) refundable ticket based on a local departure time and not what I thought was Moscow time. Why did Russia Railways take almost 30 years to change from this confusing old system?

My train, bound for Beijing, was run by China Railways, despite me travelling in a Russian Railways carriage. The timetable displayed in the corridor still showed Moscow time for stations. Perhaps changing A4 sheets of paper took time to filter down through the various levels of railway bureaucracy.

In recent years Russia had also been tinkering with its time zones, reducing the number from eleven to nine in 2011 and back up to eleven in 2014. A few time zone boundaries had also been redrawn, causing time-zone carnage online if a traveller referred to an out-of-date website or timetable.

Siberian towns were now becoming fewer and further between. I found myself spending more and more time gazing out of the window looking for any signs of civilisation. We passed a fast moving river with long, green slithers of weeds trailing in the water. Four people walked Indian file down a narrow path, along the riverbank, towards the tracks, but paid no attention to our passing train.

Outside our compartment, a man sat on a fold-down seat. He was Australian, from the Chinese section of the train, and appeared to be a little drunk. Our visitor was in his 60s, cultivated a 5-day growth, wore unwashed blue jeans, creased blue T-shirt and a greasy-looking Akubra hat. Perhaps he thought wearing such an iconic Australian hat was necessary on a long distance Russian train. Apart from letting out the occasional squeaky fart, he also occasionally mumbled to himself, or sang songs.

I tried very hard to ignore him, but couldn't help looking up when he began to sing "We're off to see the wizard, the wonderful wizard of Oz". He spotted me looking at him, and decided to invite himself over to our door, hanging onto the doorframe. He introduced himself as Mumble. "I'm sorry, what was that?" I asked. "Mumble." I'm guessing he said Murph, as in a contraction of Murphy. For the sake of argument, let's call him Murph. After an exchange of nods, he staggered away towards the Chinese carriages, never to be seen again. Thank goodness.

The passengers who joined us at Tyumen, and had been allocated compartment number 6, still hadn't settled. One massive duffel bag couldn't be accommodated under the passenger's lower sleeping berth or in the storage area above the door, so it sat on the corridor floor and blocked access to the compartment.

"Bring your bag here. I've found space for you." said Marina. The Slav dragged his bag along the corridor to empty compartment number 7, where it remained for the duration of his journey.

All passing trains sounded their horns as they tore by our carriage, at the rear of the train. Because of the Doppler effect the horns sounded like a quick "yee-oop" and our window became filled by the blur of colourful, passing freight wagons. Horns were used to warn anyone, sprinting across the tracks after we passed by, that a train was heading in the opposite direction on the hidden track.

Vagay was another monotonous, poor town, typical of many which appeared from time to time. Vagay was such an unimportant town, it didn't even appear on my detailed map of Siberia, but was important enough to include the skeleton of a large, ruined, three storey concrete monstrosity. Perhaps this had been an office block or maybe apartments, and probably a relic of the 1990s when the economy collapsed. Either way the eyesore sat unloved in an abandoned field. Our train slipped between two stationary oil trains, blocking views both left and right, adding to the gloomy nature of Vagay.

Occasionally station platform signs weren't visible, but due to the punctuality of our train, as long as I had a timetable, I could calculate what station we were at. The time was 12:11pm, which meant Ishim, an unremarkable town, but interesting to note the Kazakhstan border sat only 80 kilometres to the south. Reports of this trip in books, TV and online made me believe the scenery would be just a wall of trees on each side of the train for days, but this wasn't the case. The scenery was a blend of fields, grassland and forest, with a regular sprinkling of pine trees, birch and beech. Freight trains dominated the station at Ishim. On a parallel track, sat a train of flat cars carrying orange combine harvesters, all chained down, brand new and without wheels.

At each station stop, the same passengers left the train. Many appreciated the cigarette break, whereas I appreciated the fresh air (my mattress stunk of piss), and the chance to stretch my legs. The timekeeping of this train was impressive, and when the timetable stated 15 minutes of waiting time, we would have 15 minutes. Most passengers loitered near Marina at the end of the train, not venturing too far. For a few others, they took this opportunity to step across the tracks, made easy by the low level platforms, and visit the adjacent platform to buy drinks and snacks. Suddenly Marina called the more adventurous passengers back to our platform, as another passenger train was approaching the station, which would cut off their quick return to our train. This could have resulted in a mass no-show of passengers when our train finally departed.

Part of my regular routine saw me keeping my berth neat and tidy, smoothing out wrinkles on my mattress sheet, flicking off crumbs, and removing black hairs from the shedding woman above me.

Another break, and this time we were at Omsk (timetable: 16:36, 15 minutes), dominated by its stunning pastel green and white station building. Our train took ages to crawl out of the train yards. A set of massive locomotives passed us, pulling 72 oil tankers. Russian Railways operate around 11,800 diesel and electric freight locomotives, and each one looks massive compared with European locomotives, mainly due to the Russian broad gauge. As a result the trains are wider and also taller.

Omsk grew during World War II, being far enough away from the fighting on the European Eastern Front. It offered a well-developed infrastructure and had been earmarked to be the Soviet capital should Moscow fall to the Germans. After the war, the city remained a major industrial centre and a leader in military production for the USSR.

I stood in the corridor, watching the flatness of Siberia pass by, dominated by beech trees, broken by occasional pockets of wild grass and flowers. What was this land used for, and who owned it? My moment of contemplation was broken when a man walked up and down our corridor, looking into each compartment. He wore a tight black T-shirt and blue jeans, and spoke to me in an accent I couldn't quite pinpoint. "I've lost my wife." He didn't look too worried, just a little annoyed at this slight inconvenience. Perhaps she was still standing on the platform at Omsk, waving the train goodbye, with a cheeky grin on her face.

Approaching Barabinsk the land was billiard table flat. We were exactly 3,000 kilometres from Moscow, which I found staggering to comprehend. Barabinsk station featured two preserved locomotives, a diesel and a fine black steam locomotive, which both attracted interest from many passengers. I wanted to grab a photo or two of the locos, but as they stood at the forward end of the platform, I wasn't convinced I had enough time to make the return journey there and back to our carriage. Would the male carriage controllers on the Chinese carriages, who wouldn't recognise me, allow me to jump on board further up the train and walk to the far end? Probably, but it wasn't worth the risk, as 'probably' doesn't mean 'definitely'.

I wandered back to the rear of the train, so I could quickly jump back on board once Marina gave us the warning shout that the train was due to depart.

I tried one of the few Russian phrases, one of the few I had managed to remember, on Marina.

"Ty govorish' po-angliyski?" (Do you speak English?)

"A little." She replied.

"How far are you travelling on this train?"

"Irkutsk."

"How long do you stay there before you return back to Moscow."

Marina nodded, as a sign of comprehension. "We are there for a short break, and then return back to Moscow."

"You must miss your family being away for so long."

"Yes" she said. "I am away for nearly two weeks. I have two daughters, but my husband is there." She circled her hand as if trying to find the right words." My sister helps too."

"And then you do this all over again." I said.

"Yes. We have a saying… (she circled her hand again trying to think of a translation)… East or West, home is best."

We shared a brief laugh, which was interrupted by a station announcement in Russian, and she announced to all that we had to climb back on board.

Travelling on such a long journey gives you time to ponder, away from the worries of normal daily routines, about life's great mysteries. Take for example, instantaneous combustion. This was really big in the 1980s. I recall seeing black and white photos in magazines, showing a living room, a comfy chair discoloured by a sooty stain, and a pair of smouldering slippers by the fire side. Instead of a chalk outline of a body on the kitchen linoleum, there would be a black ash silhouette. This strange phenomenon seemed to affect people with limited mobility, perhaps through age or girth, who were unable to move once they caught fire. Strangely, no one seems to instantaneously combust on board trains, which is a good thing. It would cause carnage to their timetables. (Bing Bong. "We regret to advise a delay to the 11:00 train to Obninsk due to an instantaneous combustion incident at Kaluga. Russian Railways apologise for any inconvenience this may have caused.") In the name of science BBC set light to a dead pig in a blanket (not the food, but the real thing) in 1998, and after taking a while to ignite, parts of the pig had burned, and the bones incinerated, so it could happen, but fortunately never on trains.

How does someone go from travelling on the Trans-Siberian to instantaneous combustion? A friend once described me as having a head like a box full of frogs. That's how. With this in mind, I decided to visit the restaurant car for a bite to eat.

I wasn't hungry, due to the lack of exercise and the lack of calories needing to be replaced, but thought at least one visit was necessary. My pork schnitzel, roast potatoes and a can of Russian beer cost 850 rubles. This meal was greasy, but tasty, and the price affordable, but not something worth paying for each day. There were six other passengers in the dining car; four Spanish travellers on one side of the aisle, and a Portuguese couple on the other side. The Portuguese couple had stood close to me at Yaroslavaya Station in Moscow all those miles ago, and I also bumped into them on the overhead bridge at Perm yesterday. This couple, named Martim and Mariana, were much in love and enjoying a long distance adventure holiday together. They were heading for Ulaanbaatar, and so were travelling in one of the Chinese carriages further up the train.

"I'm interested in history", said one of the Spanish guys to me. "Especially the Silk Road. Did you know there's a car rally along this route?"

"Is that the Paris-Peking Rally?" I asked.

"No, this one requires you to buy an old car under a certain value, really cheap, and you have to drive it to Beijing. It might take a week, it might take three weeks."

"So, these old cars end up abandoned in Beijing?" I suggested. He nodded and laughed.

The two Spanish couples continued to chat amongst themselves as I tucked into my meal. Marina later walked through the dining car, and I smiled at her, and managed to receive a smile back. And who says the Russians don't smile?

In fact most people say that. For many centuries, everyday existence in Russia had been a strenuous battle for survival. As the life of the common Russian was so gruelling, worry had become an entrenched common facial expression. When did you last see Vladimir Putin smiling on the news, considering he has so much to smile about?

There seemed to be little enthusiasm when dealing with strangers. Requests for information received an answer with nothing more than a "Maybe, I guess so." non-committal sort of answer.

Russians tend not to give toothy smiles. Their preference was the closed mouth smile, as revealing too many teeth was considered vulgar. Consider a dog or a horse baring its teeth. Humans shouldn't do that.

Smiles are not seen as a form of politeness. They are considered a demonstration of insincerity, secretiveness and unwillingness to show one's true feelings. When a Russian smiles, it demonstrates the smiling person has personal affection towards the other person. Customs and immigration officers must never smile. Stop smiling and focus on your job.

If a Russian person smiles, there must be a good reason, and this reason must be known to all witnessing the smile. If the reason for a smile was not clear, Russians may worry about the reason behind it. There is a Russian proverb, which translates to 'The smile without reason is the sign of stupidity'. Smiling could be seen as a sign of certainty and confidence, so when people smile without a purpose, they might seem odd, perhaps they know something you don't, or they are about to trick you.

However, when you do receive a smile from a Russian, it can be a glorious sight. I once applied for a Russian visa through an office in Edinburgh. Behind the desk sat a stunning East European girl with China Blue Slavic eyes. It was time to play a game.

"Are you Russian?" I asked.

"No. Latvian."

"You must be used to the heavy snow we just had."

"We are not allowed to talk about the weather." She was not permitted to take part in the great British conversation starter – the state of the weather. As she represented the Russian Government, there would be no chance of building a rapport.

"You must have thought we over-reacted when we had a snow fall of just a few centimetres, and roads are closed and trains are cancelled?"

She laughed, gave a beautiful smile, and her eyes sparkled.

"Yes, we thought it was very funny." That's what I call a result.

We reached Novosibirsk at 1am, and a digital board above the platform displayed a temperature of 13°C, but the air felt much colder. In fact, after five minutes of standing in the fresh air I began to shiver, so retired to the safety and warmth of my compartment.

The town was founded in 1893 as a future crossing point of the Trans-Siberian line over the River Ob. Today Novosibirsk is the third largest city in Russia, and is located at the north end of the Turkestan Railway. Should I ever catch a train to southern Kazakhstan from Russia, this is from where I would leave.

DAY 17:
SOMEWHERE IN SIBERIA

I woke at 4:15am and even at that early hour the sun managed to sneak through the curtains. Everyone else in my cabin was still asleep. After some eavesdropping last night I determined I was the only foreigner in this carriage, with all other foreigners travelling in the Chinese carriages. At 4:15am no one used the toilet, so I could take my time, instead of feeling rushed, conscious of a line forming outside. In fact there were no other voices with all compartment doors closed. The only sign of life was Natalya in her office fixing her make-up.

As the train arrived in Irkutsk early tomorrow morning, I thought I should start sliding into the local time rhythm. This wasn't jet lag, but I wondered if such a condition as 'train lag' existed. There was a condition experienced by some long distance shipping crews on container ships, but as the crossing of time zones was slower, it was more of a 'travel fatigue' than a lag.

Our passing train disturbed a flock of crows (technically a 'murder of crows' – what a horrible expression) feeding in a field. This had been the first wildlife seen since leaving Moscow. Siberia had no shortage of trees, but no birds, so wondered where they were hiding. Descriptions of this stretch of line mentioned the taiga, the primeval uncut virgin forest. However, the land had gradually become less forested and more agricultural now. Fields were dotted with yellow bales of hay, to be used as feed during the long harsh winter ahead.

A few hours before Krasnoyarsk the land turned golden, with fields of grain ready for harvest. TV documentaries featured this route in the middle of winter with the severe temperatures experienced along the way. Viewers loved to watch TV celebrities fight off frostbite and hypothermia while standing on snowy platforms grimacing for the camera. Unfortunately they, and the viewers, were missing out on the natural beauty of Siberia in summer.

Our carriage provided three power points, all located in the corridor, and used by the provodnitsas to vacuum the compartment floors. Otherwise, they were constantly used to charge phones, which sprung into life, announced by a cacophony of notification sounds, as we entered Wi-Fi areas. Power points were limited, and as soon as one became available, there would be a rush to grab it. If you want to be the carriage hero, bring along a few Russian double adapters when you travel on this train.

Hundreds of freight cars crowded the station yard at Achinsk. Most contained fibreboard or logs, with others loaded with yellow dump trucks, colourful freight containers, oil and gas tankers and wagons containing cement. All freight yards along the Trans Siberian route seemed to be at saturation point, with only a small number of lines left free for through traffic.

As we approached Krasnoyarsk I spotted something unusual - hills - covered in a blanket of pine trees. In fact these hills average around 410 metres or 1,350ft above the surrounding river levels. One peak is an extinct volcano. The huge rock cliffs in the nearby Stolby Nature Reserve make the area a popular rock climbing location. The hills also feature a couple of ski jumps and in winter, probably no shortage of snow.

I stepped out onto the platform to buy a bottle of water from the woman at the platform kiosk. I usually wore flip-flops as they kept my feet cool, and they protected the feet, for hygiene reasons, when visiting the toilet. This time, however, I pulled on socks and my walking shoes, and noticed my feet were swollen. I also had the urge to go to the toilet, but knew this would be a waste of time. Slight constipation was another side effect of sitting for too long on a long distance train.

What a stoic expression I received from the girl selling the water. She couldn't have appeared more uncaring if she had tried, but I reminded myself this was just a 'Russian thing' and not something to be taken personally. The station building itself was absolutely stunning, made from a combination of Italian and Russian white marble and regarded by many as the most beautiful station on the Trans-Siberian line. If there was one thing the Russians did well, it was to build stunning railway stations.

During Stalinist times, Krasnoyarsk was a major centre of the gulag system, with several in the surrounding area and during World

War II (sorry, Great Patriotic War), one actually inside the city. After the dissolution of the Soviet Union and the start of privatization, ownership of large plants and factories, such as the Krasnoyarsk Aluminium Plant, switched to alleged criminal authorities and oligarchs, while others declared themselves bankrupt. Russia's economic transition resulted in a dramatic rise in unemployment and numerous strikes. Perhaps my water-selling girl on the platform found little to be cheery about.

Our train rolled out of Krasnoyarsk, and soon afterwards I spotted my first Russian farm animals; 10 cows guided by a farmer resting his stick on his shoulder. They all ignored the passage of the train. The hills in the distance looked glorious, covered in a blanket of coniferous trees, and the trackside fields sprinkled with pink wild flowers. Scenes like this always left me feeling happy and content, and then I would quickly be brought back to reality by a loaded coal trains heading west, the multi-coloured blur rattling past our window, with the usual end-of-train "yee-oop" horn.

Gansk was another depressing town, and featured a number of derelict and abandoned factories, and acres of wood chip piles, rotting in the Siberian sun. A rusty, abandoned car sat in an overgrown field. Dark, wooden houses had managed to survive the transition back to nature, despite the effects of the harsh elements rotting the walls and roofs. Permafrost also played a role in slowly destroying these structures by affecting the integrity of their foundations. Huge piles of fibreboard littered ramshackle yards and one included a rail siding with wagons loaded ready for shipment.

Ilanskaya station sat in the centre of a busy freight yard. Coal hoppers dominated the area, with wood and lumber wagons coming a close second. I stood on the overhead bridge, which linked the platforms, and lined up a photo of a stationary locomotive. Photographs from station platforms always included freight trains in the background. A freight train rumbled by and blocked my view, occupying the only free track out of ten lines. I lowered my camera when, out of the corner of my eye, approaching military trucks on flat cars came into view. How sensitive was the Russian Government when it came to photographing military equipment? Now was not the time to find out.

We eventually bid farewell to Ilanskaya, and as we rolled out of the station, dozens of Korean shipping containers sat on a line of flat wagons, an indication the 'Far East' wasn't too far away now. Ilanskaya's claim to fame was having featured as a time rift location in alternative history in the sci-fi 'Kirov' novel series. The city of Kirov was located some 2,600 kilometres to the west of here, and visited on day 15.

I wanted to see the inside of the Chinese carriages, and to see how they varied from the Russian ones. These carriages appeared cleaner and quieter. Second class carriages had carpet in the corridor, whereas the Russian carriages offered cheaper and more practical linoleum. Two of the carriages appeared to be made of mahogany, and I noticed the compartments, when discreetly glancing into them (perhaps that's why border control officers do that?), appeared plush with red velvet interiors. Did we have any first class carriages attached to this Chinese train? I managed to reach the front carriage, which was also second class, so there were definitely no first or third class carriages on this train. The Chinese portion also lacked a restaurant car, so the Russian restaurant car was the only source of food for the whole train, and it appeared to be lightly used. Two workmen, one Russian and the other Chinese, then chased me from the front carriage. This carriage was closed to passengers, with tools and rags lying on the floor. They were working on the pipes underneath the boiler at the end of the carriage, and seemed less than keen to have a nosey foreigner standing in the way staring at them.

Returning to my compartment, I found mum and Alex mid-meal, tearing chunks off a loaf of bread, and placing a little dead fish on each one. This combination was stuffed into their mouths. Until now their diet consisted exclusively of dried noodles and large pickles, sliced in two lengthways, and sprinkled with salt.

I started to wonder whether the smell of piss was coming from the mattress of Alex's mum, and not my mattress. A waft of piss smell would arrive each time she moved on her seat. After giving the subject more thought than it probably deserved, I came to the conclusion many lower berths were subjected to this pissing treatment. Why Russians wet themselves on board trains remained a mystery unsolved, unless, after a heavy day of drinking, they lost control of their bladders, and possibly their legs as well.

Experiencing the sheer size of Russia made me wonder whether a population scattered across such remote places, was a burden on the nation's economy, as well as creating a political and also geographical disconnect with Moscow. Did the people of Siberia feel little relationship to Moscow and the Kremlin, despite the Trans Siberian Railway linking them with European Russia?

Anton Chekov wrote as he travelled across Siberia, "My God, how far removed life here is from Russia." A similar feeling exists today, with Siberians relying on themselves and each other, rather than Moscow.

Almost three-quarters of Russian exports come from Siberia and yet the sheer size of the region, its extreme climate and misdevelopment, holds Russia back. Wealth extracted from the ground was shipped to European Russia, and in exchange Siberia received revolutionaries, dissidents, criminals and prostitutes.

To highlight the way Moscow treated Siberia, gas was extracted from the land and pumped west. Meanwhile, Siberians burned brown coal to keep warm, which not only harmed the environment, but harmed humans as well.

In one recent tax year, the Tomsk region raised 130 billion roubles of tax revenue, and received back only 10.3 million. Tyumen provides Russia with two thirds of its oil and 90% of its gas, but receives such little in return, it has to rely on subsidies from Moscow.

The main highway linking western Russia and Siberia is an unreliable stretch if bitumen, notoriously flood-prone in spring and autumn. This explains why the more reliable Trans-Siberian Railway received such high investment from the Russian government.

In a recent poll in Irkutsk, 80% of respondents said the current Russian regime, in one shape or form, was seen as their enemy (of which 41.5% specified Putin). In comparison, China only received 2% of the vote.

Siberians generally believed Moscow exploited them. Apart from providing most of Russia's wealth, the region was also seen as an important photo location when Putin wanted to be seen fishing or riding horses shirtless... and not much else.

An Irkutsk historian and sociologist once summed up feelings here when he said "All Siberian cities had different problems, but they had a common grievance against Moscow." From time to time the idea of Siberian independence had been discussed in hushed voices. There was an underlying feeling Siberia could survive without Moscow, but Moscow couldn't survive without Siberia.

In 1992 Siberia took its first tentative steps towards independence by developing a local currency and printing banknotes. The less than snappily-named 'Internal Financial Transaction Units' looked similar to US dollars, apart from the portraits of the US president. It was fairly unlikely the notes would have featured the image of then-President Boris Yeltsin. A total of 2.5 million IFTU's were printed, but the First Chechen War in 1994 and Putin's unwillingness to even talk about breakaway republics scuppered the idea of Siberian independence. Even Wikipedia's Siberian language section disappeared mysteriously.

An independent Siberia did once exist, but only for 122 days, back in July 1918. After this short spell of freedom, the region was absorbed back into the USSR after the Russian revolution.

Vladimir Putin recently began an ambitious scheme, called the 'Far East Hectare' program where land was given away in Siberia in an attempt to boost the population. Unfortunately for Putin, the scheme hadn't quite worked the way intended. Instead of European Russians relocating to Siberia, it had only encouraged them to build a second home there.

220 million hectares of land had been made available for the scheme, but only 80,000 Russians took up the offer. The State would offer a grant of 1.5 million rubles (US$20,000) if an actionable plan for land development could be offered. Unfortunately for the Government, Russians prefer European Russia rather than the marshes and mosquitoes of Siberia.

We rolled into Tayshet, whose name literally meant 'cold river' in the Ket language. If the town ever had a tourism push, swimming might not be the number one attraction. Founded in 1897 Tayshet became an important supply point and station on the Trans-Siberian

Railway. From the 1930s until the 1950s, Tayshet was the centre of administration for the gulag labour camps called Ozerlag and Angarstroy. Today Tayshet seemed a much happier place. Here was the junction for the new BAM railway, which skirted the north of Lake Baikal, and terminated at Sovetskaya Gavan, opposite the island of Sakhalin.

After Tayshet, heavy pine forests dominated the landscape. With nothing of interest outside, I focussed my attention across the compartment. Mum and Alex had been wearing the same clothes for four days. Alex wore a grey T-shirt and Hawaiian board shorts. Mum wore a flowery top and ¾ length jeans.

Sunset in Siberia tonight left the white birch trees along the side of the railway line appearing to be on fire. In a break between the trees, I spotted an outhouse at least 100 feet from a farmhouse, and imagined how challenging this would be in the middle of a Siberian winter when nature called. In another break between trees, two men swung petrol-powered strimmers, clearing a field of over two acres, on a job, which would keep them busy for some time.

Across Russia, immaculately uniformed staff stood on station platforms and watched the trains go by, holding a baton vertically to indicate all was well. The Baton Brigade weren't just seen at stations, but stood at bridges and other strategic points, including important level crossings. Considering the size of Russia's rail network, there must be thousands of staff standing around all day just watching trains.

I later researched the number of staff employed by Russian Railways – a staggering 740,315 at the last count – but still a drop in the ocean compared with Indian Railways with 1,308,000 employees. Despite 18% of the world's population living in China, Chinese Railways employed only 285,405 staff, probably due to the country embracing technology.

At around 9:30pm, the train pulled into Zima. Mum and Alex quietly left the cabin, and we gave each other a farewell wave.

This must be a great place to visit in the middle of a Siberian winter, as Zima (зима) is a Russian word for 'winter'. Another Russian word for winter is год, pronounced 'God', a word that may enter your mind as you step off from the train onto the platform at -40°C.

Zima was situated on a low-lying, water-logged plain, which made it an important stopping-off point for pond, bog, fly and mosquito enthusiasts. The local 'continental' climate saw air temperatures varying between a rather chilly −45°C (−49 °F) in winter to an equally unpleasant +40°C (+104 °F) in summer. Tripadvisor posts seemed to focus, not on what to do in Zima, but more importantly on how to leave the place.

Zima was the first Russian town to appear on my Mongolia-China map, with Irkutsk just one sleep away.

The empty berths opposite didn't remain empty for long, being occupied by an old woman and her daughter, both with Mongolian looks. Two incoming mobile calls arrived during the night, waking everyone up in the cabin, giving us the opportunity to enjoy the old lady's loud and animated conversations.

This section of track was the scene of a massive derailment just months earlier. Around 300 metres of track were torn up and overhead power lines brought down when 29 coal wagons were derailed. This stopped all freight and passenger services on the Trans-Siberian route for just eight hours. I find that incredible. Considering how remote parts of the line are, and the amount of work required to fix the track and overhead lines, a repair in eight hours is simply amazing. Here in the UK, should a line be affected by a landslip or major derailment, you can expect the line to be closed for weeks. It's amazing how quickly a repair can be made when it's vital for the national economy or reputation.

DAY 18
IRKUTSK, RUSSIA

We were just one hour from Irkutsk so I decided to stand in the corridor and soak up the remaining portion of this amazing train ride. I gazed out of the window, and in a huge, overgrown field, five domestic-looking dogs ran around in a pack sniffing the ground and each other. Later, I saw another four dogs, noses to the ground and their tails wagging. When Russia hosted the 2018 World Cup, unofficial estimates suggested up to two million stray dogs lived in the 11 host cities. However, no official statistics exist on the number of stray dogs in Russia as a whole, and experts were not sure either. This was not a recent phenomenon. Russian writers, such as journalist Vladimir Gilyarovsky, first mentioned Moscow's feral dogs in the late 19th century.

One effect of the large feral population was a high and rising level of dog attacks on humans. In 2007 official statistics suggested 20,000 attacks took place, of which 8,000 required police or medical intervention. Much of the aggression came from dogs living in forested areas, which were poorly socialised and more prone to aggressive territorialism.

On the bright side, Russians generally agreed feral dogs kept cities and towns free of food leftovers and kept rat populations down. In Moscow feral dogs have adapted to urban life and understand the rules of traffic lights and even ride the Metro. They are often called 'Metro Dogs'.

I decided to give dogs in Irkutsk a wide berth, fighting the temptation to scratch one on the head while saying, "Who's a good boy?" My outcome may not have been the same as rubbing the statue of Ingus the dog, at the Moscow Metro station, five days ago.

The rumble and flash of a passing train broke my thoughts. This train hauled flat cars loaded with tanks, complete with snowploughs, followed by my first Chinese language shipping containers.

Recent reports announced wild Amur tigers were falling victim to canine distemper. The virus caused muscle twitching and confusion, and eventually fatal seizures. These wild dogs carried eight species of tapeworm, six species of roundworm and seven species of flatworm. Also, feral dogs had no fear of trains. A small pack prowled right up to the edge of the tracks as our train rumbled past. These dogs were best avoided.

I've always thought the crapiness of a phone's ringtone was directly proportional to how long it took to answer the phone. The worse the ringtone, the longer the owner took to slide the phone button and mumble "Hello?" As we approached Irkutsk, phones came alive as we entered a Wi-Fi area. Phone-starved passengers rushed out of their compartments to check their phones charging in the corridor.

Did spells of no Wi-Fi reception, for those addicted to their phones, experience similar withdrawal symptoms as people without cigarettes or drink? A recent survey in the UK of 2,000 people revealed almost 6% regarded losing their phone a serious stressful life event, more serious than a family death, imprisonment, losing your home or terrorist threats. That could explain why most passengers drank heavily or just lay on their berths and napped. They couldn't think of anything else to do when there was no Wi-Fi reception.

IRKUTSK, RUSSIA

I was excited to arrive at Irkutsk. The Ibis Centre Hotel had been reserved, but since the train arrived at 7:13am and the hotel had a check-in time of 2pm, this gave me two options. I could turn on the charm at the reception desk and ask for an early check-in, or at least store my backpack in a storage room, and explore Irkutsk in a 4-day unwashed state.

I asked for an early check-in with the man at the reception desk, explaining how wonderful a shower would be, having just stepped off the train from Moscow. The odds of having an empty room, so early in the morning, in the middle of the summer season would be slim.

"Let me see. I might be able to do something at 9:30am if you can wait?" I nodded enthusiastically. He gestured in the direction of the buffet breakfast area, which was a hive of activity, with dozens of conversations, the smell of cooked breakfasts and clinking of plates and cutlery filling the air.

"Help yourself to a coffee or a breakfast while you are waiting." I couldn't believe my luck and didn't hang around in case he changed his mind, so thanked him and stocked up on an overdue coffee and breakfast without the added rocking motion of a train.

A young woman, standing behind a lectern, checked room numbers from guests as they walked into the breakfast area, but decided to go AWOL just as I arrived. I tucked into my breakfast, with my large backpack sitting by my side, and when she returned, she never questioned my motives. She did see me, but must have assumed I was about to check out and was enjoying my final breakfast. In actual fact I was doing the opposite. Guests aren't entitled to a breakfast until the morning after check-in. Thank you Ibis, and thank you Accor. To be honest, some of the luck may have been down to my Le Club Accor frequent guest membership. That was not a paid endorsement, but I believe it's handy to have hotel memberships... just in case.

After washing off four days of grime, I felt a burst of energy, also helped by escaping captivity from a train. On my way out I handed the helpful man at the front desk a bar of Cadbury's chocolate and a packet of Scottish shortbread brought along from the UK. He looked at these in amazement. "I really appreciate you arranging the early check-in," I said. "You helped me so I want to thank you." He was speechless. (The following day he left a 'Thank You' note and a small badge featuring the Irkutsk coat of arms on my room table!)

In actual fact I brought the shortbread and chocolate along for the provodnitsas on the train. I had read offering the carriage attendants a gift was a nice gesture, to thank them for all of their hard work, and making the trip memorable. Unfortunately for Natalya, she was busy barking at a passenger when I disembarked at Irkutsk, so she missed out.

My exploration of Irkutsk resulted in me walking 28 kilometres/17 miles. My train-induced cabin fever over the last four days encouraged me to walk, and walk even more. I gained a few blisters. In fact, my feet were wrecked from walking on the hot pavements for most of the day, and I also managed some sunburn - in Siberia! Russians believed sour cream, yogurt, and kefir made dry red skin soft, smooth, and supple. I chose not to try this remedy out, since the smell might have attracted feral dogs.

During my walk around Irkutsk I visited an ornate church called Sobor Bogoyavlensky, and obediently obeyed the 'no photography' sign, despite a desire to photograph the stunning interior. Russian Orthodox churches are simply amazing. They are like Roman Catholic churches, but on steroids, and they were doing bling before bling had a name. A group of Chinese tourists shuffled around the church, and appeared not to understand the pictorial signs indicating 'no photography', and snapped away.

Irkutsk had many impressive churches, monuments and sculptures, but I found only one tourist shop, selling overpriced local honey, carvings and vodka aimed at the Chinese market. The shop sold no postcards, no vodka miniatures (perhaps Russians wouldn't stop at just one shot, making the idea of a miniature bottle of Vodka a ludicrous idea), no stuffed Siberian tiger toys, and nothing tacky. This was very disappointing.

With my feet shouting at me, my last port of call, before heading back to the hotel, would be the main railway station. Today marked the anniversary of the arrival of the Trans-Siberian railway to Irkutsk. An impressive black steam locomotive sat by the platform, with a neat line of children and adults waiting to climb on board and pose for photos. Adjacent to this, on a parallel track, sat a green heritage diesel, and next again a modern, state-of-the-art electric locomotive. The ornate teal and cream station building was adorned with red, white and blue bunting. Had they been tipped off I was passing through Irkutsk? Unfortunately not, as these colours also belonged to the Russian Federation flag.

Outside the station a band performed on a temporary stage in the car park. A cordoned-off area, in front of the stage, had been reserved for invited guests only. Just because I had travelled 10,300 kilometres to be there wouldn't necessarily make me a VIP, so resigned myself to standing behind the rope with everyone else. A five-piece band banged out a repertoire of Russian tunes, which were much appreciated by the locals in the audience, with some dancing to the music as if no one was watching.

I wondered what locals did to fight off boredom in Irkutsk, in the middle of winter, when temperatures dropped as low as −49.7 °C. One constructive way was highlighted at an Irkutsk landfill site. Workers built a medieval fortress from scrap metal and refuse from their garbage dump. While looking online under the search 'boredom in Irkutsk', Google's predictive search feature offered 'boredom in Irkutsk crossword clue'. Google uses a predictive search algorithm based on - wait for it - popular searches. You can read into that any way you like. ("Let's see…six across, twelve letters. I know… TundraTedium.")

While researching another project, I found an interesting article from a newspaper dated 1847. The article centred around part of the entertainment on offer at Yakuti weddings. Yakuti people lived in the modern day Republic of Sakha, located northeast of Irkutsk. This spectacle involved a man and a youth gorging themselves to bursting point. Together they were offered a staggering 36 pounds (16kg) of boiled beef and 18 pounds (8kg) of melted butter. The man was described as having his 'skin hungrily hanging in loose folds over his gaunt bones' while the youth relied 'chiefly on the vigour of youth and a willingness of disposition.' After gorging on the beef, they used a ladle to grease their throats with melted butter ready for the second part of the competition.

They managed to devour around half of the meal in just one hour. 'Their eyes were starting from their heads, and their stomachs projecting into a brace of kettledrums.' said the article. They somehow completed their meal, and they remained for 3 or 4 days in a state of stupor, neither eating or drinking. They were rolled about on the floor, which some believed, helped their digestion.

Boredom in Irkutsk? Don't you believe it - not with entertainment like that. Now I know what inspired the American TV program 'Man vs. Food' starring Adam Richman.

DAY 19:
DAY TRIP TO LAKE BAIKAL, RUSSIA

I planned to stand in the waters of Lake Baikal, which seemed to be a good idea at the time, considering I might never be there again. My train from Irkutsk to Slyudyanka was bound for Vladivostok, and I had been allocated a seat in a second class compartment. In the upper berth lay a man who laid still for the whole duration of my journey to Slyudyanka. Opposite me sat a woman, and her ginger-haired daughter, Vika. This berth also smelled of piss, and the stink was much stronger than the train from Moscow. Fortunately this journey would be only three hours in length.

The scenery was remote and rugged, with wooded hills, steep valleys and even a railway tunnel – the first I could recall seeing since France. As we rose in elevation, a thick fog enveloped the train. Two hours into the journey, while photographing an approaching tunnel through a dirty corridor window, our provodnit (male) waited by my side. After our noisy passage through the tunnel, he decided to talk to me in Russian. As a result of this unsuccessful communication attempt, he left me alone, and I breathed a sigh of relief as I had perhaps broken a Russian Railways by-law by photographing railway infrastructure.

He returned after five minutes accompanied by a provodnitsa (female) from an adjoining car. Her limited English didn't help, and she coaxed me into my compartment and we sat down. The other occupants watched with fascination, no doubt thinking, "This will be good." She showed me her battered, official train timetable for Russian Railways, which was about the size of a Thomas Cook European timetable. How would I get my hands on a copy of this fascinating book? Her timetable showed the same arrival time in Slyudyanka as my printed e-ticket, so what was she trying to tell me? I looked at my watch, pointed at the arrival time on my e-ticket, and she kept speaking in Russian. Suddenly she broke into English, "You station thirty minute."

By now Slyudyanka was just twenty minutes away, but finally the penny had dropped. Despite being aware of the arrival time, staff we away when the music stopped. This was a good thing, as I would have re obliged to remind me to get off the train. I stepped onto the platform at Slyudyanka, and thanked the provodnitsa (she smiled!), and shook the provodnit's hand, offering him a "Spasibo".

Two employees insisted on warning me of my approaching station. There may have been ramifications if this crazy tourist had missed his station, but that was another example of Russian friendliness. Despite Russian and foreign Governments perhaps not getting along, the people always appeared warm and helpful towards foreign visitors.

Slyudyanka station overlooked a busy rail yard, crowded with boxcars, coal and assorted wagons ready to move. It appeared to be a typical Russian town, with a colourful Orthodox Church, dogs roaming the streets (domestic, not feral) and drivers not knowing what indicators were for. Today was Sunday, and a large number of women congregated outside the beautiful wooden Church of St. Nicholas. All of the women wore scarves over their heads, and many held young babies, suggesting a mass Christening was about to take place inside.

After the heat of yesterday, today bordered on chilly. An angry breeze swept across Lake Baikal, making the water choppy and the waves slap against the concrete erosion wall. Around two dozen visitors stood on the lake shore, either photographing the horizon ("Look at my photo. Look how the grey water merges into the grey sky.") or taking selfies with the same monochrome background. I seemed to be the only person silly enough to take this further, by actually standing in Lake Baikal. Yes, the water was cold, but the worst part involved walking over the large pebbles, on blistered feet, to reach the water's edge.

Most visitors approached Lake Baikal further along the northern coast at the town of Listvyanka, which had all the trappings of a tourist trap on Google Streetview. Alternatively, on the other side of the Angara River, lay the village of Baykal. Day tours departed from Irkutsk, which would include a ride by train on the remaining section of the original route from Baykal to Slyudyanka. Sadly no tour operators would accept a single traveller! The original portion of the old line was built between 1902 and 1904, and included 39 tunnels and numerous bridges. There would be a number of photo opportunities, and one tour even mentioned time to take a swim. This option would have been unpopular today.

Or maybe not. Russians are famous for their tolerance of swimming in cold and icy water. Even Vladimir Putin has been filmed taking an icy dip. Unless viewers can lip-read Russian, what he mutters under his breath, while dunking in the freezing water for the cameras, can only be guessed.

Lake Baikal and the surrounding ecosystem have over 1,000 species of plants and 1,550 species and varieties of animals. Over 60% of animals are unique to the area and of the 52 species of fish in the lake, 27 are found nowhere else. Lake Baikal is a flooded rift valley, where portions of the Earth's crust are pulling apart. At the deepest point, the lake bed lay 1,186 metres or 3,893 feet below sea level. This was my favourite Baikal statistic - under the water was an incredible seven kilometres or 4.3 miles of sediment. That was a seriously deep crack on the Earth's surface. Today I stood in its freezing waters (albeit briefly).

Many Russian stations featured preserved steam locomotives. They were not only a nod to the country's railway heritage, but were popular attractions for visitors. Britain began passenger rail transport back in 1807, when the Swansea and Mumbles Railway at Oystermouth carried passengers in horse-drawn carriages on an existing tramline. Unfortunately I couldn't recall one single preserved locomotive outside any UK station or on a platform. Why were our locomotives locked away in stuffy, cramped museums instead of outside where the public could enjoy them?

In the back of my mind I knew the answer, but asked a work colleague anyway, who was seriously into trains. She thought the problem might be space. Russia has lots of space, whereas British train stations are located in crowded city centre sites offering little space for static displays. And anyway, Network Rail would rather use any available space as a car park, raising revenue, rather than embracing the historical significance of railways in the development and prosperity of cities and towns.

Omul is a whitefish species of the salmon family endemic to Lake Baikal, It's served smoked, and not being a fan of smoked fish, I would normally give this a wide berth. However, when in Slyudyanka...

The little shop on the station platform stunk of smoked fish. A gust of fishy stench hit my nostrils at the doorway. I purchased a slab of fish, which was prised open with a few thin strips of wood, and took it to a platform bench to enjoy. And my opinion? Omul tasted of smoked fish. I was reminded of my Dad and his love of kippers – a herring split, salted and smoked over smouldering wood chips. He also loved 'Arbroath Smokies', which were hot-smoked haddock. Either way, once dried, a great deal of time was required to pick out the flesh. My father would spend about a week working through each fish, carefully picking out each morsel of meat from between the bones. Eating these fish was a form of culinary surgery. I would watch him, and not grasp the joy gained from this operation, as the time-spent versus the meat-gained ratio made no sense to me.

I wanted to see the Yuri Gagarin statue by the side of the busy P-258 road, so walked the short distance out of town. The statue was easy to find, but it wasn't in a safe location to loiter, especially with crazy Russian drivers speeding by. I'm not convinced Gagarin had a connection with Slyudyanka, but his statue was here all the same. There was also a statue in a small park by the lakeside, called 'Pamyatnik Slava Trudu' (Glory to Labour monument), which also featured proud Soviet workers and a cosmonaut. The 1960s must have been a great time of immense pride in the Soviet Union, as leaders of the space race.

Many Russian drivers appeared to be, how shall I say this, a little reckless. Just outside of Slyudyanka sat the 'Monument to Bear and Monkey', a white painted concrete sculpture, located by a bend on the P-258 road. This piece of art wasn't placed here as a cultural reference, but as a barrier to prevent speeding cars from careering into a vital utility pole and a traditional wooden house located just behind. The utility pole was reinforced by two concrete poles, but these were obviously deemed insufficient. I often watch trashy TV programmes featuring car accidents – many show footage from dashcams – and many of these have Cyrillic script times stamped on the images. In fact a large proportion of video clips seem to originate from Russia and countries from the former Soviet Union. Dashcams are popular in Russia, with the footage used as evidence to support the driver's innocence when someone, as drunk as a skunk, ignores a red light and slams into your car at full speed. This could be another reason why level crossings in Russia include Hostile Vehicle Mitigation road blockers.

I booked a 3rd class seat on my train back to Irkutsk, just for the experience. Photos on the internet and videos on Youtube convinced me there would be limbs hanging out of berths, a strong smell of humanity, and half-expected to find chickens flapping around the carriage. Imagine my disappointment when the carriage wasn't a sleeper, but a respectable, warm and comfortable 3rd class seating car. Most passengers had Mongolian faces, the carriage was filled with music, children playing, chattering and a hint of communal life, which was a lovely surprise.

DAY 20:
IRKUTSK-ULAANBAATAR

This morning's rain wasn't heavy, but inconvenient enough to leave me damp after a 20-minute walk from the Ibis Irkutsk Center Hotel to the station. At least I'd taken advantage of my buffet breakfast before checking-out.

I expected this train would be made up of bland, green Chinese carriages, as its arrival time into Irkutsk was the same time as my arrival from Moscow two days earlier. Ergo, it must be the same type of train made up of the same type of rolling stock. However, this train was composed of modern Russian carriages. Our compartment felt narrower than the train from Moscow to Irkutsk and the toilet also felt more cramped. This modern design managed to squeeze in another compartment by saving six inches here, six inches there...

A skinny Spanish girl, named Angela, had been allocated the berth above me, and a French couple, named Iriane and Bastien, occupied the berths opposite.

Before I had a chance to fling my backpack onto my lower berth, a friend of Angela asked if I would mind swapping my berth with her berth, three compartments along the carriage, since they were travelling together and had been split up. More likely their reservations had been booked separately and as a result were allocated random berths. I'm always happy to help if possible (being the carriage hero and all that), but she held an upper berth, and I preferred (and paid for) a lower berth. Despite her chocolate brown eyes and attractive smile, I wasn't prepared to sacrifice my lower berth.

By staying put, I did Iriane and Bastien a favour, as these two girls never stopped talking. Angela spent most of her time in the other compartment, and their Spanish conversation drifted along the corridor almost non-stop all day.

I made a pleasant discovery - this compartment didn't smell of piss. Being an overnight, international service and not a domestic run, I guessed getting drunk wasn't a necessity. All passengers in this carriage

111

were tourists, all completing the Trans-Mongolian route, except for one lone Russian man.

I covered the first section of this journey yesterday during my day trip to Slyudyanka and Lake Baikal. Low lying cloud and the general gloom of the Primorsky Range made the scenery less than inviting, but today, under the sun, the region looked splendid. Even at this eastern extremity of Russia, freight trains still rumbled past every four minutes, filling the left window with a colourful blur of passing coal and oil wagons.

Mongolian arrival cards and customs forms were handed to each passenger within an hour of leaving Irkutsk. No sense in leaving things until the last moment, despite the border being more than eleven hours away. I decided to wait and complete the paperwork at Slyudyanka, where we would stop for a few minutes. The lurching of the train made completion of the forms almost impossible, as Iriane found to her grief. Her forms looked as if they had been filled in by someone having a fit.

Lake Baikal looked blue and calm today, as the train skirted the southern shore. Iriane tried to find our location with a mobile phone app. "I can't get anything. There's no Wi-Fi." she said.
Not to make things too obvious, I politely waited a few minutes before unfolding an item called a map, and carefully traced our route.

Later on, Iriane and Bastien enjoyed their lunch of rehydrated mashed potatoes and rye bread. I fancied a small bottle of white wine, crackers and a cheese platter, to complement the beautiful blue Lake Baikal views outside the window, but my packet of soup and can of preserved fruit would have to do. Considering the difficulty of finding canned fruit in Moscow, I may have been the only passenger tucking into this sort of snack in our carriage.

We followed the shore of Lake Baikal for hours, passing spruce and fir forests. Eventually, the train turned away from the lake and headed inland, through grasslands, beech forests and seas of yellow wild flowers.

Bastien napped continually and only rose to have lunch with Iriane. This couple wasn't used to travelling together and facing separation at the same time.

112

The train followed the wide Selenga River for about an hour, until we changed direction and crossed over an impressive bridge – actually one of two truss bridges. Our bridge heading south sparkled silver in the sunlight, whereas the other, for northbound traffic, was a rusty red. We followed a wide, flat valley, bound by forested hills on each side. The scenery was complimented by the sound of Angela and her friend yakking in Spanish further down the corridor.

Outside, the scenery began to change and even the pine trees looked different – my first Korean pines – and I spotted my first yurt in the outskirts of Ulan Ude.

Wearing shorts and flip-flops was a convenient and comfortable option when travelling on this train. The digital display in the corridor indicated an outside temperature of 22°C, however on the platform at Ulan Ude, the air felt decidedly chilly.

I spoke to a man from Ireland named Patrick. He asked where I had travelled from, and said Moscow, being a deliberate ploy to avoid questions and strange looks.

"I started in London." he said. "I caught a train to Paris, then to Brussels, Berlin, Moscow, Ekaterinburg and then Irkutsk."
"That's some journey." I replied.

I wasn't prepared to turn this into a competition, so avoided mentioning my Vila Real de Santo Antonio to Ho Chi Minh City adventure ("My journey's longer than yours!"). I also didn't want Patrick considering me as crazy, or to burst his travel bubble. Patrick's compartment was towards the front of the train, and so probably wouldn't see him again unless we bumped into each other at the border formalities.

While we loitered on the platform at Ulan Ude, a change of engine took place, from an electric to a diesel locomotive. The sight of a distant diesel locomotive belching out a trail of black exhaust would now lead us into Mongolia.

I felt fortunate not to be staying further down the train near Patrick's carriage. At Ulan Ude dozens of Chinese school children, all wearing identical red sweatshirts, poured onto the platform. They stood in small groups having their photos taken, chased each other around the platform or just messed around as children do.

Like many locations along this line, the area experienced a population explosion after the Trans-Siberian Railway arrived. The line opened here in 1900, but the town remained closed to foreigners until 1991. Ulan Ude's claim to fame was the huge statue of the head of Vladimir Lenin sitting in the central square, which was claimed to be the largest in the world. Whether it was the world's largest *head* statue or the largest head statue of Lenin wasn't immediately clear. For head statue enthusiasts, it is 7.7 metres or 25 feet tall and weighs 42 tons.

ONBOARD DRINKING

We had a few new faces in our carriage now. Two men stood in the corridor, bathed in sweat and out of breath. Later, while walking along to the hot water boiler at the end of the carriage to cook my noodles, I quickly made 'border security' type glances into each cabin. Life seemed to become rowdier further along the corridor. Four talkative Malaysians sat in one compartment, the following had four rather loud Chinese men drinking from Heineken cans, Angela and her friend sat talking in Spanish, and at the rear compartment Russians were becoming slightly drunk on local brew. Each compartment had a 'no drinking' sign inside, located above the door, which seemed to be universally ignored.

It's important to mention this boiler is called a boiler. It's not a samovar, as mentioned online and in some guidebooks. Russians use samovars for heating water for tea, and they say they are old, antique boilers heated by wood. Never insult Russians, and their tea culture, by saying you will add boiling water to your noodles from a samovar.

The challenge with Russian long distance train travel was surviving the long time spent on the train. Travelling by train was cheaper than flying, but the mind-numbing monotony, of days and nights in the same train, could be overcome by passengers getting drunk and falling asleep. Drinking was so ingrained in local culture, Russians used a word describing a drinking binge which lasted several days –

запой (zapoy). This journey had been so enjoyable with the scenery so novel. However, if this journey had to be made on a regular basis, I'm sure the monotony would eventually wear me down, and might even become a victim of zapoy.

I don't drink vodka, but enjoy the occasional beer. In 2011 the Russian Government signed a bill officially classifying beer as alcoholic. Until then any drinks containing less than 10% alcohol in Russia had been considered a foodstuff. Although vodka had long been the traditional tipple in Russia, the popularity of beer had soared in recent years, marketed as a healthier alternative to spirits. Over the past decade, beer sales in Russia increased over 40% while vodka sales fell by nearly 30%. Russian alcohol consumption was still twice the critical level set by the World Health Organization.

25% of Russian men died before reaching 55, in comparison with 7% of men in the UK and about 10% in the United States. The average life expectancy for men was 66 years, placing Russia among the lowest 50 countries in the world.

In 2018 state statistics agency Rosstat announced Russians born in 2017 were expected to live 72.5 years on average. This improvement was thought to be due to the impact of the economic transition in the 1990s and a decrease in risk-taking behaviour among men, such as drinking and smoking. However, the older generation, born in Soviet times, still had the lowest life expectancy.

While in Moscow I visited a cemetery, and noticed a trend where headstones featured an engraving of the deceased's face. Most of the photos, on which the engravings were based, showed the subject in their more attractive youth or in their physical prime. One grieving family had struggled to find a suitable photo, and used the best photo they could lay their hands on. The man in question appeared to be using his left hand to support his head, as he nodded off to sleep at a kitchen table. The high number of graves belonging to young men aged 20-22 years were disturbing, with the remainder dead by 60. This was an unfortunate result of the male Russian lifestyle.

In 2016, 61 Russians died from drinking bath lotion used as a liquor substitute. President Putin responded by cutting the excise taxes on alcohol, in an effort to cut the demand for surrogate options. He also pushed for tighter regulation of the manufacture and sale of any product containing more than 25 percent alcohol. Irkutsk saw 11 arrests tied to methanol (methyl alcohol), a toxic chemical occasionally called wood alcohol or carbinol. Methanol was believed to have been in a lotion called Boyaryshnik, which came from hawthorn berries. Boyaryshnik was often used as a vodka substitute due to its high alcohol content. Sadly, almost half of the victims were women.

Methanol is also used in antifreeze and to produce formaldehyde and a number of other products. In 2012 a similar outbreak occurred in the Czech Republic, traced back to counterfeit vodka and rum bottles found to contain methanol. This lethal booze was made using windshield wiper fluid imported from Poland. In the middle of a Siberian winter, entertainment could be limited, and so drinking cheap booze was a solution to help block out the long months.

I read a newspaper article from 1870 of a local Schismatic gentleman whom, through prayer, fasting and a great deal of scripture reading, decided to save his soul by crucifying himself. The article reported he was only partially successful, and I could imagine why. Unless he received help, self-crucifixion would have been impossible. This genius may have been under the influence of Boyaryshnik when he devised this cunning idea.

After departing Ulan Ude, the land turned more desolate, void of trees, and featuring just dry, scraggy shrubs. Cattle grazed by the unfenced tracks and the train driver frantically honked his diesel horn to scare them away.

We passed Lake Gusinoye, a huge fresh water lake 24 kilometres long and 5 kilometres wide. The surrounding land was almost treeless, giving the lake a barren and mysterious appearance. Did the Soviet Union deliberately tried to ruin scenery? A seriously ugly power station, dominated by two tall red and white chimneys, had been built back in the days of the USSR and still dominated the area. Since the motherland came first, the Soviets didn't give a toss about the environment. These eyesore chimneys continued to be seen for over ten miles, occasionally poking up in the distance from behind grassy hills.

RUSSIA-MONGOLIA BORDER

Before the border crossing, our provodnitsa pulled all window blinds down halfway – "Russian tradition!" she said, and we all laughed. The reason may have been to prevent illegal items being 'accidentally' dropped out of the top of the window.

Due to my 'frontieraphilia' (a love of land border crossings), I find border crossings novel and exciting, as the EU offered freedom of movement and no hard borders. As any border crossing, involving Russia, was bound to be exciting, I looked forward to leaving from Russia with love, and entering mysterious Mongolia. I had read a few horror stories, and countless tips, but this is what actually happened:

19:55 Arrive Naushiki station (Russia).

20:05 Uniformed officials entered the train.

20:09 We were subjected to a head count followed by a second head count.

20:11 Our passports were taken away.

20:15 The fun now began. There are six uniformed staff in our carriage, all looking grim and in various coloured uniforms and Soviet-style hats. We are instructed to stand in the corridor. One man, sweating profusely, opened a hatch under the corridor carpet, revealing a compartment we didn't even know existed. Another officer opened all of our storage compartments (maybe looking for smuggled Fabergé Eggs?), followed by a sniffer dog. One Russian female with a 'don't mess with me' look about her looked at me and said "Good boy, go in." and gestured to go into the compartment. Before I had a chance to give her my filthiest look, I realised she was talking to the dog – in English! Now, this always happens to me - I'm always singled out. The 'Don't mess with me' woman then definitely snapped at ME "Go into cabin and show me your bag!" I was more than happy to comply with her kind request, so did as ordered. Every pair of eyes from our compartment watched me from the safety of the corridor and thought, "This will be good."

"Show me your bag." she snapped again. Perhaps she realised I was deliberately slowing down just to annoy her. I dragged my backpack out from under the seat. It was me versus the Russian Government, and they didn't stand a chance. "Open please." She said 'please' (a little respect works wonders with me), so I opened the top of my rucksack, releasing any trapped odours, and she immediately looked away, perhaps her sense of smell was as acute as her dog's. "Open these." she said, pointing at the storage compartments behind each headrest. "Open this." she said, pointing at the headrests of the French couple. I thought to myself "God, I hope they don't have contraband in here. By the way, where the hell is everyone?" She seemed satisfied and left me alone, marching to the next compartment to torment another passenger. Everyone calmly returned to the compartment, while I sat on by berth slightly traumatised, but feeling I had won a small battle against Putin's Government by annoying that official.

21:02   A new engine was attached to the train.
21:05   Russian uniformed staff began drifting back to the station building.
21:12   Passports returned.
21:45   Our train rolled out of Naushiki.
21:59   We crossed the border, marked by a high wire fence, topped with barbed wire and illuminated by floodlights. Was this to prevent Mongolians from entering Russia, or to stop Russians from leaving? I wondered how far the border fence ran, so once home I checked Google satellite images, and it appeared the entire 3,452 kilometre Russia-Mongolia border was fenced, with a wide, cleared strip of land on the Russian side.
22:25   We arrived at Sukhe-Bator station (Mongolia). Bastien frowned and asked, "I wonder what we are in for now?" I replied "I think they will be laid back. Nothing will get past the Russians, so the Mongolians will be more relaxed." I don't know what he was anxious about, as I'm the one always singled out.
22:34   Our customs cards were collected.
22:46   A passport control officer appeared at the compartment door, and our passports were taken away.

23:00 A soldier walked through the train, glancing into each compartment.

23:52 Our passports were returned by an immigration officer who welcomed us with a "Welcome to Mongolia." and a smile.

00:12 Our train left Sukhe-Batar.

The total time to cross the border lasted 4 hours and 17 minutes, and the toilet was locked for the duration. In fact, our provodnitsa had locked the door 30 minutes before arriving at Naushiki.

Angela, the Spanish girl, was the only casualty in our carriage. She spent 30 minutes in an office and eventually returned to the carriage unnerved.

"My Mongolia visa was issued for a Portuguese citizen and I am Spanish." she said. There were five or six others with problems."

"Did they accept your visa?" I asked.

"No, they issued a new one".

"Did they charge you for it?"

"No, they did it free."

Today's lesson was invalid visas will be rejected at the border, but re-issued if possible. I couldn't believe the Mongolian Consulate in Spain would confuse a Spanish passport holder for a Portuguese citizen, so guessed she had arranged her visa through a third party, and that's where the error arose. Fortunately border staff were happy to help Angela. EU nationals can't usually obtain visas at a Mongolian land border, so the officials had been understanding and accommodating. I'm sure if Angela had tried to enter Russia from Mongolia, the outcome would have been very different.

After the excitement of a border crossing, and waiting in line for the toilet, I tried to squeeze in a short sleep before our arrival in Ulaanbaatar.

DAY 21:
ULAANBAATAR, MONGOLIA

I woke to a glorious sunrise and a clear, blue sky over a treeless landscape. This was the mesmerising Mongolian scenery seen on travel documentaries and in brochures. Anyone with a camera or phone vied for a chance to photograph the iconic Mongolian train photo. While our locomotive hauled the carriages around bends, we all tried to grab a shot of the train ahead, without the blur of a passing telephone pole in the foreground.

With just six thousand UK arrivals each year, I felt very privileged to visit Mongolia. Visitors generally spent their time trekking, climbing, bird watching, horse riding, rafting, camel riding, yak caravaning and joining overland motorcycle tours. My plan involved doing none of the above, and since Ulaanbataar wasn't seen as a city break destination, I would definitely be the odd one out. No change there then. According to the Ulaanbaatar Tourism Department, only 1.3% of visitors arrived from the UK in 2017, with over half of all visitors arriving from neighbouring Russia and China. Even Australians outnumbered the Brits.

We arrived into the busy Ulaanbaatar station on time. Tourists blinked in the dazzle of the morning light, and perspiring men in soaked T-shirts pulled trolleys of boxes along the platform.

For the second time on this journey, I thought about chancing my luck with an early check-in at a hotel. When in Irkutsk the Ibis Hotel couldn't have been more helpful. Could I be this lucky again at the independently run Voyage Hotel? Whether they would allow me access to a room at 7:15am, when check-in was from 2pm, only time would tell.

The smiling girl at reception looked at her monitor, and a few moments later said "Yes, no problem." I could have jumped over the counter and hugged her, but I was tired and dirty, and also didn't want to compromise my good luck. I wasn't offered a complimentary breakfast this morning (I didn't expect to be offered one, but can live in hope), so happily paid for one. At just 10,000 Tugriks (£3.50) this was not just convenient, but a bargain as well.

I was offered a huge bedroom – in fact the largest room allocated to me so far on this journey. I was also pleased to hear the train whistles from the station across the road, as if I hadn't had enough of assorted train noises already. Unfortunately the continuous honking of horns from the traffic outside could also be heard.

Showered and unpacked, my first priority was to find the office of Selena Travel and to collect my train ticket to Beijing. Despite Google Maps' notorious reputation for questionable accuracy, I eventually stumbled across their office. The collection details supplied to me included a Google map of the area. The map showed one side street where the office should be, but unknown to me there were two parallel streets, adjacent to each other. I wandered up the first one, and ended up in a housing estate, much to the confusion and eventual entertainment of local children playing in the street. Once I found the second street, the travel agency was easy to find.

My feet ached again today, having walked 28 kilometres. While walking the streets, admiring UB's modern architecture, I couldn't help but be amazed by the local's driving skills, or more specifically, the lack of them. I actually considered asking my new friend at the Voyage Hotel reception desk whether a Highway Code existed in Mongolia, similar to the UK. This guide explained the road rules and courtesy to be used when behind the steering wheel. I saw no evidence of such a driving code in Ulaanbaatar.

Cars in Ulaanbaatar are modified and have their horns connected to their brake pedals and accelerators. Any reason to slow down and the horn is blasted. If the driver in front makes a random U-turn, he will receive horn blasts from multiple drivers. If a driver tries to make a left turn from a right hand lane – horns. Oops. Someone just realised they didn't have a clue where they were heading, and chose to change lanes without indicating – horn. Change lanes while indicating – horn. My favourite moment occurred when the traffic light changed from red to green. Hesitate for a nano-second too long, and a napping motorist will cop a series of horn blasts from the drivers behind. An online guide to driving in Mongolia stated a 'sound signal may be used only to prevent traffic accidents or warn other drivers during overtaking on roads outside of built-up areas'. Being inside a built-up area, the constant use of horns on UB roads must be to warn others of a potential accident every 10 metres.

My thoughts on the subject were broken by a loud exchange of horns, so decided to slow down and watch the entertainment. "This will be good." I thought to myself. Picture this scene: a lady driver, in a silver Toyota needed to change to the right hand lane and indicated her intention. Perhaps she thought by indicating this automatically entitled her to the right of way. The man in the black Mazda decides she can go fuck herself, as UB drivers don't give way to anyone. She received an angry honk for daring to switch lanes in front of him. She stopped, stuck her head out of the window, and, I guessed, wished him a very light sleep tonight. He honked his horn again. She nudged forward and stopped deliberately to annoy him, but the event fizzled out without any further excitement.

There are a high number of imported Japanese cars on the roads. This means a high number of motorists driving in right hand drive vehicles on the right hand side of roads. This may account, at least partially, for the inability of drivers to drive in an internationally recognised fashion.

Pedestrian crossings were another interesting aspect of walking in UB. Unlike in the UK, when stepping onto a pedestrian crossing, traffic should stop, Ulaanbataar drivers were expected to totally ignore pedestrians and possibly even accelerate, while honking their horn. Crossing a road on a zebra crossing reduced your chances of death by only 5%. The more pedestrians crossing in a group, the higher your survival rate, but not by much. Tip: always have someone between you and any approaching car, just in case. Pedestrian crossings also have green crossing signals. These still offer no guarantee the approaching traffic won't try running the red light, as obeying red lights at crossings appeared to be only voluntary. If I was foolish enough to step onto a road when a driver was obviously accelerating to run the red light, then I must accept the consequences.

Even stopping or pulling over for a speeding ambulance appeared to be voluntary. The situation was so chaotic, ambulances came equipped with loud speakers, so the driver could broadcast a kind request such as "Good Sir, could you make way for us at your earliest convenience, as we are in a hurry?" I'm assuming this was the gist of the announcement.

Five people said hello to me today, and they were all middle-aged or older men with ruddy complexions, who were perhaps no stranger to the occasional 12-pack of local Sengur beer. One even saluted me. I have a tendency to march and not stroll or saunter. I'm definitely not a saunterer, so along with my camo shorts he perhaps thought I was ex-military. I even had a Chinese visitor ask me for directions!

My feet were throbbing, so I planned to have a lazy night, with a meal at the Voyage Hotel Mongolian restaurant. Imagine my disappointment when I hobbled in at 8:15pm to learn the restaurant closed at 8pm, with the place looking like the Mary Celeste in partial darkness. Outside, a loud thunderstorm raged, turning the streets into torrents. Fortunately I had bought a tub of noodles for my train to Beijing, and the room included a kettle, so I dined like a sad bastard on my own, watching throat singing on Mongolian TV, and ate a dish loosely described as chicken flavoured noodles.

My hotel window had an insect screen in place, so I decided to leave it open overnight to let some cool air in. Unfortunately it also let in the incessant honking of horns and at least one mosquito. Mongolia is known for its enormous mosquitoes. She probably thought she'd won the lottery dining on a yummy European. It may have been the taste of the chicken flavoured noodles coursing through my veins she enjoyed. I woke to several red throbbing, itchy spots on my left leg and one on my right hand, all swollen and the size of a fingernail. Hopefully she died of food poisoning.

DAY 22:
ULAANBAATAR, MONGOLIA

Another day in UB and another day of UB's unique driving skills. At one particular busy intersection, a frantically whistling traffic policeman waved a red baton in a feeble attempt to control the traffic, despite traffic lights in operation. He was attempting some resemblance of order, since few drivers seemed to take traffic lights seriously. Unfortunately no one seemed to take the traffic policeman seriously either.

I paid a visit to the Gandantegchinlen Monastery today. Outside the entry arch, hundreds of shitting pigeons flapped about in a feeding frenzy. Happy adults and children fed happy pigeons, resulting in the ground turning into a mass of grey feathers, beady orange eyes and thrashing wings. Pigeons are rats with wings, but for Buddhists, feeding pigeons brings good karma. In Buddhism, serving others, without any expectation, was the hallmark of the purest form of compassion. However, by feeding pigeons, you know you will receive pleasure and good karma in return, so was this not contradictory?

A bus passed slowly by in the heavy traffic and the driver honked his horn. One hundred pigeons simultaneously rose in the air in a chaotic mass of wings. Naturally they decided to fly in the same direction – towards me. Feeling the disturbance of the air on my face caused by their flapping wings, I ducked for cover behind a tree until the coast was clear, much to the amusement of many children.

Inside the monastery stood a gold, 26.5 metre high statue of Avalokiteśvara, dozens of prayer wheels, candles, and an entire wall of dolls, all identical except for the colour and design of their cloaks. The peace, devotion, incense and calmness felt wonderful, and if there had been a place to sit, I would have stayed longer, or perhaps just stayed permanently, with the thought of writing a travel book just a distant memory. While soaking up the tranquillity, I wondered what the teachings of Buddha said about patience, respect and compassion, and why UB drivers didn't incorporate this into their motoring skills.

Mongolian television is fairly dire. Channel TV9 offered a cultural program about traditional guitars and throat singing. We don't get this sort of entertainment too often on the BBC. During the commercial break an advertisement left me with my mouth open. The advertisement appeared to be a government information service, like the ones broadcast in the UK years ago. They told us how to cross a road safely, why we must not drink and drive, and why we must wear a seatbelt etc. This television commercial was brilliant, and much more interesting than the throat singing. This advertisement promoted the importance of politeness. To be honest I had met nothing but politeness while in Ulaanbataar, but the Mongolian Government thought there was still scope for improvement.

Picture this scene: a woman is mopping a floor in an office building. A man asks if he can walk over her freshly mopped area. She agrees, they exchange smiles, and the world, or at least Mongolia, is a better place.

We then had the crowded elevator scene: the elevator arrives at the desired floor and the young lady at the back needs to squeeze out. She smiles and asks to be let out. The handsome young man by the door steps out to give her space. They exchange a sort of pre-coital smile as she steps out of the elevator.

The driver scene: I thought to myself, "This will be good." A young man in a car realised he was in the wrong lane. What a silly man. He says out of his window, "Excuse me Miss. Sorry for the inconvenience, but due to a momentary lapse of concentration, I have found myself in the wrong lane. Would I be able to cut in front of you? I could have leaned on my horn like other drivers, but it's nice to be nice." Our smartly dressed young woman in the desired lane says back, "Of course you can. It is my personal pleasure to allow you to cut in." They exchange smiles. In reality however, the scene would have featured an exchange of honking horns and the man saying "Let me cut in!" She would reply, "I was here before you, so kiss my ass, and maybe in future prepare in advance, fool." while leaning on her horn in return.

Buddhists believe in Karma and reincarnation. Based on the way UB motorists drive, most motorists will come back in a future life as yaks. Mongolia has a population of only 3 million, but with an estimated 640,000 yaks, I may be onto something.

Let's return to the monastery. A man, with a good grasp of the English language, stood outside selling nick-nacks. He held out a small palm-sized snuff bottle, which had the appearance of silver and amber, but the soldering gave away its true age. I had found it difficult to find a decent souvenir, as gifts in UB seemed to be dominated by slippers, Mongolian fur hats, horse statues and 'How good is my driving?' stickers for car rear windows.

"How much?" I asked.

"Twenty dollars. I will also take Mongolian Tugrik."

"Sorry, I haven't enough." I showed him a fist of notes worth around five dollars. He wasn't interested.

"I have Russian rubles." I said, in a matter of fact way.

His eyes lit up. "I take rubles too."

I began to walk slowly towards the monastery. He said "1,500 rubles!" This calculation came rather quickly so made a quick calculation of my own - close to the $20 mark.

I rummaged in my bag and pulled out a 1,000 ruble note. "This is what I have." I lied.

"OK, deal," he said. We both left happy. I don't haggle well, but left happy as the price had been knocked down by one third without actually trying.

He decided to show me a collection of old coins, but I wasn't interested. He soon bid me farewell, and disappeared into the crowd, after earning enough to feed his family for several days. I have no problem with haggling, but when the saving is just a dollar or two, what's the point? What's more important, saving a couple of dollars or saving precious time in a fascinating city?

Fast food restaurants are avoided when travelling, but when I need fast food, air conditioning and a place to sit, restaurants like Burger King had their place. Inside Burger King, on the corner of Beijing Street and Tokyo Street, I approached a Danish man and his girlfriend and said, "You're a long way from home. Did you ride all the way from Denmark?"

"Yes I did. " he said. "How did you know I was from Denmark?"

126

"I saw your bike outside with the Danish number plate." He smiled, and nodded his head in acknowledgement of my Sherlock-like skills.

These intrepid travellers had ridden across Eastern Europe, across Russia and into Mongolia.

"How long did it take you to cross Russia?" I asked.

Oh, let's see... about 19 days. " I pitied his poor girlfriend clinging onto his motorbike for almost three weeks.

"What were the roads like?"

"They tend to get worse the further east you travel." he said. "We couldn't ride into China. You need a sponsor who will travel with you, and that was too much trouble."

"How are you getting home?" I asked.

"We will ride back into Russia, and visit Kazakhstan and Uzbekistan."

"How have you found riding around the streets of UB?"

He laughed. "It's quite an experience!"

They had total freedom, and the ability to be self-reliant. My journey was weak in comparison. Climb on board a train, make myself comfortable by the window, and let a train driver take me to my next destination.

Mongolia is not a rich country and city bosses lack the funds to lay proper pavements, or to maintain gifts offered by other countries. Near the base of the Zaisan Monument sat a golden Buddha, so I decided to take a closer look. A small flight of steps led up to the base of the statue, but they had fallen into disrepair and were roped off. The area was overgrown, and exuded a sense of abandonment. The 18 metre-tall Buddha and grounds had been a gift to the people of Mongolia by the South Korean Government in 2007. Why had this impressive and interesting attraction, a place of prayer and reflection, become nothing more than an uninviting and overgrown piece of spare ground? If this was in the UK, the area would have been taken over by locals by now, forming a community action group called 'Friends of the Buddha Gardens' or something, and it would be looking immaculate.

My feet were now throbbing from another long day's walk, so returned to my hotel. That's when I noticed a touch of class in my room.

127

Next to my kettle and sachets of coffee, sat two teaspoons, both stolen from Russian airline Aeroflot. Nearby lay a small notice, for the attention of all guests, which I translated from Mongolian to English using a phone app. One read: "Use your utensils with the right culture. Please note that there is a charge in case of stains, leaks or loss that cannot be removed by washing." This was a reminder either not to use chopsticks for the consumption of soup, or Westerners should stick to our normal cutlery, and not to be too cocky with chopsticks. Another notice read "Use bed linen neatly. In the case of strong soaking, which is impossible to wash and spoil, you will have to pay the cost of bed linen. I wish you a happy journey." I prefer not to consider how a bed sheet could become so stained it would have to be replaced.

TV travel documentaries have a lot to answer for. I have seen a few colourful, well-directed shows where the travelling celebrity slept in a ger or yurt and showed little obvious inconvenience or discomfort. He or she will enjoy the hospitality, sipping fermented mare's milk ("Wow, this is really good.") while smiling and nodding approvingly to the host, and appearing to enjoy an entertaining evening of monotone throat singing. "Tomorrow morning we will catch a few wild horses, and maybe milk a yak, so it's off to bed now."

All documentaries followed the same script when in Mongolia, making viewers feel these were mandatory requirements when visiting the country. Full engagement with the country didn't happen unless visitors caught a live session of throat singing or spent a few nights in a yurt. I didn't come to Mongolia to live the life of a nomad, but to catch a train to Beijing.

To emphasise this point, visitors to Scotland don't spend their vacation in a rustic, thatched roof bothy on a windswept stretch of shore. What percentage of foreign visitors to the USA stay on an authentic ranch? Travellers to New Zealand don't live with sheep farmers, and backpackers to Switzerland don't stay on a dairy farm halfway up a mountainside. I'm trying to justify my total and complete lack of interest in how Mongolian yurt-dwellers live, and in particular a keenness to avoid fermented mare's milk.

DAY 23:
ULAANBAATAR TO BEIJING

Mongolian Railways operated our train today, the cleanest train experienced on my entire journey so far. Imagine the luxury of a shower at the end of the carriage, spare rolls of toilet paper, paper hand towels, a bottle of liquid hand wash and air freshener. Also, our carriage was almost entirely made up of Dutch people.

I shared my compartment with a Dutch woman in her 50s who occupied the berth above me, and a Dutch man in his early 20s on the opposite, lower berth. His travelling buddy returned home early after losing his passport after a drunken night out in Novosibirsk. I found further down our carriage an Australian man, and a Chinese woman and her young son, but all others seemed to be Dutch. It was all rather odd.

The Mongolian landscape was bleak, but mesmerising. Rolling hills of green grass dominated. There were no trees or bushes, but just grass, swaying in the breeze. A falcon took off from a trackside telephone pole, scared by our passing train. In fact it's common for ravens, buzzards, falcons and kestrels to use trackside poles as an observation point and also as a nest-building site, due to the lack of trees.

Approaching Choir, the landscape became drier and flatter, and we learned from our provodnitsa we wouldn't be able to stay on board for the bogie change at Erlian. All passengers and their luggage would be removed from the train. Travelling into Mongolia may have been different, but heading into China, with their rigid customs and immigration formalities, it would be a case of "Everyone off!"

This was disappointing news as many reports had mentioned the bogie change from Mongolian broad gauge to the Chinese standard gauge, and I really hoped to experience this. A huge grabber lifted each carriage off the track, the bogies were rolled away, and replaced by bogies of a different gauge.

I still wondered about the abnormal number of Dutch passengers in this carriage. The woman above me was named Brigette and the young man Gijs, who reminded me of tennis player Andy Murray. Brigette was a tour leader for a Netherlands-based tour operator, which explained why we had so many of her countrymen on board. There had been one or two German conversations in the corridor as well, and I mentioned this to Brigette. "We have a few Germans in our group as well. " she laughed.

The two languages sounded quite similar. I know basic (very basic) German, and could often work out the flow of conversations drifting from the corridor, whether in Dutch or German.

The scenery was now semi-arid, with more soil or sand than grass, and what did grow, was a dusty grey-green shade and no more than a foot high. In such a remote location I was sickened to see plastic bags caught and tangled along the trackside fences, and plastic bottles by the side of the tracks. I couldn't believe travellers would throw their rubbish out of windows, especially in such a barren and ecologically sensitive area.

Our last station before the border was Sainsand, where we could leave the train and stretch our legs for 30 minutes. Stepping down from our air-conditioned carriage onto the platform, the dry heat immediately hit me like a sledgehammer. The glare from the sun was blinding, but I decided to reach the front of the train and see the brute of a locomotive hauling us towards China. I began to wilt after 15 minutes, so wasted no time taking photos and heading back on board. What a forlorn place. Only a special type of person could live in Sainsand, and to my surprise over 24,000 souls did.

Two hours from the border, the land was parched, with the ground dominated by sand with sprouts of struggling grass. Welcome to the Gobi Desert.

Our train crawled into Dzamyn-Ude (Mongolia), and we passed a stationary Chinese train. There seemed to be a lot of excitement directed at our train, with dozens of passengers and crew all grinning and waving at us. When did you last see passengers on board a bus wave to other bus passengers? This was also to happen at Datang the following morning. Compared with the military green blandness of the Chinese carriages, our modern white and lilac train must have been an eye-opener to the Chinese travellers. And then border formalities began.

19:12   (22 minutes late) We arrived at the Mongolian border station at Dzamyn-Ude. Excited passengers filled the corridor, and the air was full of the sounds of the Dutch guttural language. The buzz continued until a blue uniformed official passed through the train. He said to us all, "Sit down please." As he said 'please' we did as requested. While in Irkutsk I couldn't find any decent souvenirs, but did manage to bring something special along with me - a bout of diarrhea. What I didn't need was the need 'to go' with toilets securely locked up to 30 minutes prior to arrival, and after leaving stations – or while sitting stationary at a border check-point.

19:27   Our passports were collected.

19:42   Two military officers in grey and white camouflage uniforms walked through the carriage. I nudged Gijs and said quietly "Why do they wear such camouflage on board our train? It's not very good. We can still see them." They peered expressionless into each compartment as they passed, like all border officials do.

19:50   Our customs declaration forms were collected.

20:30   Our passports were returned.

20:40   The train rolled out of Dzamyn-Ude.

21:05   The train arrived at the Chinese border point of Erlian, and we were all ordered to leave the train with all of our possessions. LED lights lit the station up, and music played from platform speakers. This was a nice touch and a gentle introduction to China.

21:10   We joined the customs lines.

21:30   We cleared customs, our luggage was scanned through an x-ray machine. When passing through the green 'nothing to declare' channel, I wasn't challenged. An immediate visit to the toilets found only Asian cubicles, and no paper. This could have been a serious disaster if I hadn't brought along my own supply. This was the first time (and only time) on this entire journey my own toilet paper would be used.

21:35   We all sat in the waiting room as a locomotive shunted our train away for a bogie change. I spent the following 2½ hours listening to an elderly Australian and an Englishman comparing travel adventures. These two men had covered the same territory in Africa.

"Do you remember the bus station in Bujumbura?" asked the Australian.

"Sure do, but that was a palace compared with the bus station in Kigali."

They both nodded slowly, and looked at the floor, reflecting on what must have been a challenging and traumatising episode of their lives.

00:15   We were allowed back onto our train.

02:00   The train departed Erlian.

A number of Youtube videos showed traders bringing goods across the border by leaving them in passenger compartments, but this didn't happen to us between Mongolia and China. Like the bogie change, this entrepreneurial maneuver was probably directional.

DAY 24:
INNER MONGOLIA, CHINA

I woke at 7:15am, after 5½ hours of disturbed sleep. On two occasions Brigette's blanket fell off her upper bunk and landed on my leg, which hung out of my berth. I squinted out of the 3 inches of window not covered by the blind, and saw bright sunshine, a dry, eroded land, and the fact our train was making good speed.

We arrived at Datong dead on time. On the opposite platform sat a bland, military green Chinese train, and its passengers and crew showed us more than a fleeting glance. Windows were filled with waving hands, and smiling faces. A few adults stepped onto the platform to photograph our train, followed by the inevitable selfies. Gijs asked me what the excitement was all about. I suggested our sleek, modern white and lilac train from Mongolia had caused a minor sensation, compared with their utilitarian Chinese carriages. This may have been the first non-Chinese train they had ever seen, and they appeared to be well impressed.

Gijs had his nose in his Lonely Planet guide, and mentioned we would soon see a section of the Great Wall of China. Right on cue, it appeared. We couldn't see any detail, since the wall sat miles away, but on a distant range of hills a stone wall could be seen snaking its way upwards. Poplar trees grew in great numbers by the tracks, making a photo of the wall, in the gap between the passing trees, impossible.

China was a remarkable sight, being a clash of modern and traditional. Clusters of ancient houses sat side by side, all with terracotta roofs and crowned with solar panels. We passed under a number of partially built high-speed railway lines. These massive concrete viaducts sat unused, waiting for the overhead wires to be hung into place.

China planned to rule the world in high-speed trains, and currently operated 65% of the world's lines. China was still a poor country (although getting wealthier each year), with up to 80% of long distance journeys still carried out by bus. However, an increasing number of Chinese travellers are now affluent enough to afford China's

133

world-class high-speed train network, while arriving at their destination in a fraction of the time.

By giving the top portion of some corridor windows a good tug inward, I could hang my arm out of the window and photograph a classic 'train ahead negotiating a bend' shot. However I was taken aback at the heat outside, and quickly realised Beijing's heat and humidity would be a challenge. Even the trackside rail workers were taking things easy, in their hi-viz yellow jackets, standing or squatting in the shadow of stone walls, watching the train go by.

"Do you think we can access Google maps in Beijing?" asked Gijs.

"I doubt it. You can't get Facebook and many other sites because they are banned. That's why I brought my own map."

Brigette asked to photograph my central Beijing road map with her phone, since China's censorship hadn't crossed her mind either. Word spread about the lack of Google in China, and passengers from the adjacent compartment also asked to photograph my map. The carriage hero had struck again.

An A4 book was passed from compartment to compartment, requesting feedback on the comfort and cleanliness of our carriage and the efficiency of our provodnitsa. Mongolian banknotes were placed between the pages. Either this feedback book was a requirement, or a cunning ploy to assist travellers to offload their unconvertible Tugrik notes onto a hard-working provodnitsa who could use them. Either way, I thought it was an excellent idea.

We passed a stretch of hills covered with hundreds of solar panels. They looked hideous, and ruined an otherwise beautiful vista. However, the hills faced in the right direction, they weren't used for any other purpose, and solar panels placed there ensured valuable agricultural land wasn't wasted. This would never happen in the UK, but here in China, the Government has ultimate power.

Our train passed the large Guanting Reservoir, and unknown to me, this would be the start of the most spectacular stretch of track on my entire journey. On the far shore sat a collection of white buildings, which appeared to be a holiday resort. After passing through a tunnel, the train sped past an impressive dam and wound its way along even more impressive scenery along the Yongding River Gorge. Gijs said there were 66 tunnels, according to his Lonely Planet guide. Craggy outcrops towered above the train, while below, white rapids broke a green-brown river.

After passing through a long, cool tunnel, we emerged into blazing sunshine, and I noticed a sudden change in the flora. Plants with larger leaves now dominated the trackside foliage, suggesting a region of heavier rainfall. Overall, the land looked greener and more lush, leaving the semi-arid climate of Inner Mongolia far behind.

After we left the scenic splendour of the Yongding River Gorge, the horror of Beijing's outskirts began. One moment we enjoyed views of rocky crags and majestic peaks, and the next electricity pylons, concrete high-rise apartments, freeways, power stations and red and white striped chimneys, belching smoke.

Thirty minutes before arrival at Beijing, Brigette began to prepare for disembarkation. She decided to change her clothes. Gijs had disappeared to snap photos out of the corridor windows, so Brigette took her top off, revealing a fine sight indeed. I popped my eyes back into their sockets. After putting a bra on, she slipped her shorts off, slipped on a pair of green lace panties, and the shorts went back on again. Be cool, Manson. Be cool. I just pretended to read my paperback, but for the life of me I couldn't recall what book I held in front of me.

Beijing main station appeared busy in an organised sort of way. The building was as huge as an airport terminal, but by following the swarm of new arrivals I quickly found the exit. They always knew where to go.

My hotel was located just along Beijing Station West Street, but walking even that short distance, with a backpack, ensured I was soaked in sweat on arrival. I stood at reception in a pool of my own perspiration, and fanned myself with my street map of Beijing. You can't do that with Google Maps, can you? While I stood there, looking as if I had just completed a marathon, guests around me were cool, calm and comfortable, and the girls behind the reception desk just gave me sympathetic smiles.

My room wasn't quite ready, so the smiling girl at reception asked me to wait 15 minutes. I made myself as comfortable as possible

135

on a soft bench in the reception area. Rivulets of sweat trickled down my back and into my bum crack. The men on either side of me shifted over slightly, giving me more room.

Once in my room, my bags were roughly unpacked and the contents piled onto chairs. The shower felt amazing, and against my best plans, lay down for five minutes, and woke up 1½ hours later.

I had to face the heat and humidity eventually, so headed outside for room snacks. I found what appeared to be a small supermarket, with a strange English-language name, called 'Family Love', with a façade in hot pink. What an odd-looking shop. Either something had been lost in translation, or this shop might not meet my supermarket expectations. A gorgeous Chinese woman in a hot pink, short dress, leaving not much to the imagination, entered the shop at the same time as me. My initial reaction was Family Love may have been an undercover brothel, but the shop was indeed a small supermarket, and part of the Beijing learning curve.

Inside Family Love I looked for beer (a can of Tsing Tao cost 3.50 Yuan, or 20 pence). It was important to remain hydrated in your hotel room after all. I also stocked up on dried fruit (also 3.50 Yuan per packet) and biscuits. The woman in pink seemed to be following me, and this wasn't wishful thinking. She stopped next to me at the biscuit aisle. Why would an attractive woman, dressed in a way to make a grown man weak at the knees, need a packet of biscuits at 8pm? She took a great deal of interest in the biscuits on the lowest shelf immediately to my left. She squatted down and her dress rode up, giving me a view, which almost made me drop my cans of Tsing Tao beer. (Don't worry readers, I managed to catch them just in time.) Maybe there's more to this Family Love than first realised.

Beijing's streets lacked the traffic noise and honking horns experienced in Ulaanbaatar, but the complete lack of sign abeyance was up to par. Crossing a road, with walk signs and a zebra crossing markings in front of me, seemed a good idea at the time. The walk sign changed colour from red to green, so I began to cross. This didn't mean I had the right to cross. Nope. This meant I had consciously chosen this time and place to die. Cars, electric motorbikes, mopeds and scores of bicycles worked their way through the pedestrian mass crossing the road. Locals should have been more savvy and stood their ground, but usually gave way to the traffic even though they had the right of way to cross. Life was too short wasting time contemplating road crossings in China, so soon learned just to barge into this traffic. Locals would then follow *me*, and the traffic would stop and give way. This game of 'chicken' almost backfired once when I almost had a one-on-one with a man on a bicycle. There must have been karma, as he almost fell off his bike as he frantically swerved to avoid me at the last moment.

I noticed at red lights, cars stopped, but mopeds and bicycles rarely did. Were they exempt from the road rules? Also, if the roads were busy, mopeds just used the pavements. If I had to dive out of the way to avoid an accident, it was obviously my fault for walking on the pavement in the first place.

Not only were the roads and pavements of Beijing dangerous for pedestrians, but in an attempt to reduce the terrible smog problem, a serious government push encouraged the use of electric scooters and motorbikes. Some electric scooters are as cheap as US$100 with second hand models even cheaper. A recent report stated the silence of these bikes increased the chances of a collision with a pedestrian by 40%. Electric scooters in Beijing were stealth death machines.

To my excitement I found many great places to eat within a kilometre or two of the hotel. This is how I saw the situation - any place selling Chinese food, fell under the category of a 'great place'. I stood outside a couple of crowded restaurants to learn the routine when entering and ordering. Did customers order at the counter and sit down or take a seat and wait to be served? Many restaurants had a counter, with pictures of the meals and descriptions located on the wall behind (think McDonalds or KFC). Menu displays rarely included English text or menu numbers, so how would I place an order – unless I had a laser pointer. How does one differentiate between duck entrails in black bean sauce and pig testicles with noodles? Most of the pictures remained a complete mystery to me, as most of the courses were cooked in deep fried batter. One restaurant featured an incredible 192 meals on it's rear wall! If Gordon Ramsay ever visited this place, he would have a fit over the size of the menu.

Unlike the streets of Ulaanbaatar, horn honking was kept to a minimum, but this didn't mean the streets were quiet. Music blared from shops and girls stood in shop doors shouting at passers-by through megaphones. There's no such thing as a quiet walk around the streets of Beijing. I spotted small groups entering a shopping centre and thought it would be fun to follow them and see what the attraction was. The shopping centre consisted of six storeys of cramped walkways, narrow shops, neon signs and blaring noise. I decided things were quieter out on the street.

In one gloomy, quieter stretch of road, where trees and bushes cast shadows over the pavement, sat a woman. The light from her phone illuminated her weather beaten face. She looked up and gave me 'the look' and immediately realised, although illegal, prostitution was alive and well in the Chinese capital.

In another dark area, this time by the Novotel Beijing Xin Qiao, a petite woman appeared from the shadows and whispered "Hello Mister. Massage?" I declined her kind offer.

Walking past the front door of the Novotel for a quick look, I noticed the hotel gave all room guests a complimentary pair of stylish white slippers, with the 'Novotel' brand name emblazoned on the front. I had found free hotel slippers in other hotels, but the thought had never entered my mind to actually use them, never mind drop them into my suitcase with all of the shampoos, body wash bottles, hair caps and anything else not nailed down. Not all guests share this view however. Two Chinese men stood outside the Novotel's front door puffing cigarettes while wearing their complimentary white slippers. In fact the following morning at breakfast, I witnessed a serious fashion faux pas. A woman helped herself to the buffet dim sums, wearing hotel branded slippers acquired from a stay at another hotel. There's a time and a place for this and a hotel restaurant at breakfast time isn't one of them.

I sipped my Tsing Tao beer and wasted time channel hopping in my hotel room. On offer were 68 TV channels, with a handful in English, including CNN, HBO, CNBC, Bloomberg and a couple of foreign channels broadcasting in English. I found no BBC, RT, or any channels from South Korea or Japan. CCT, the Chinese Government Station, offered 15 channels, BTV had 10, and dozens of one-off random channels.

138

DAY 25:
BEIJING, CHINA

Rain had fallen overnight, leaving puddles in the car park below my window. The grey, overcast sky made me realise there would be no direct heat on my pale skin today, but the humidity would be hell.

I made myself familiar with Beijing South Station, and the connecting Metro trains. Once you've sussed one Metro, you've sussed them all. The sheer size of the station and the number of people inside surprised me. Passengers scurried in all directions, although occasionally some would stop in their tracks without warning, and cause instant tailbacks. They would look around, look where they had come from, and without warning veer off on a tangent.

I found crossing from the north entrance to the south entrance a logistical challenge. I feared bumping into someone, who had suddenly stopped in front of me, causing me to miss my pictograph and directional arrow. Keeping in mind the main directions were in Chinese, and English language words were small and of a lesser priority, I was heartened to see so many Chinese passengers also disorientated. It wasn't just me.

Locals also struggled in the high humidity, bathed in sweat, soaking backs, sweat dripping down faces, with anything remotely flappy used to create a draft on their faces. It wasn't just me struggling. The high humidity reduced evaporation from the skin, which resulted in unpleasant rivulets of sweat running down the centre of my chest and also down my back.

Outside the station two men sprinted past me. As I turned around to watch the excitement, these plain clothed officers grabbed a man, pulled his shirt over his head, and slapped his wrists into a pair of handcuffs. The poor man was led away by the officers, to face an uncertain fate. No one else stopped to watch. This was either a common event, which didn't justify stopping in your tracks and gawking like I did, or suggested a fear of State security, where paying too much attention might be a bad thing, and you might be the next person to be whisked away.

Today I witnessed technology, which could only be described as mind-blowing. Who comes up with these ideas? I was standing in a Metro car, minding my own business, staring at the flashing lights on the distant metro route map displayed at the end of the car. An advertisement caught my eye through the window opposite me and then disappeared. As we were underground I must have imagined the whole episode. After we left the next station, there it was again – a digital advertisement filled the entire window. A few stations later the penny dropped. Imagine LED hoardings, similar to the ones around the pitch at a football ground, attached to the inside of a tunnel. The impressive part was the LED images zipped along at the same speed as the train, which made the advertisement appear stationary. Seriously impressive, until the train began to slow, and the window advertisement equilibrium was temporarily broken, or by crossing a bouncy section of track, and the ad appeared to move up and down in comparison to the window. No matter, I was most impressed.

Once brought down from technology heaven, I realised I was the only European passenger in this carriage. Most adults paid no attention to me, but children were fascinated, staring at me, almost daring me to do something. I also realised something about the Chinese today – few seemed to wear watches. Perhaps Beijingers were more laid back than Europeans or could Europeans be more time conscious? More probably, the tech-savvy locals relied on their mobile phones for the time.

I'd love to see the UK adapt more of a Japanese mentality on time keeping. When a Japanese train is a minute late, the head man of the railway company greets all passengers at the platform exit with a bow, in a genuine show of apology. More than five minutes late and the railway chief is close to committing Seppuku. This system would quickly weed out much of the UK's unnecessary railway management structure. Instead of a lame excuse about wrong sorts of leaves on the track, or wrong type of snow, we would make space for a manager with genuine sorrow. I couldn't imagine a senior executive of LNER bowing in apology to delayed passengers on their arrival at the concourse of London Kings Cross station because the 11:27 from Newcastle arrived

10 minutes late.

The time had come to do important tourist stuff, so when in Beijing, high on the agenda was a visit to Tiananmen Square and the Forbidden Palace. Metro trains were a sanctuary of cool air conditioning, but every time we arrived at a station, and the doors slid open, a gust of warm, sticky air blew into the carriage, negating any good the air conditioning had achieved.

Total chaos ensued at Qianmen Metro station. Hundreds of passengers disgorged from my train, and we took ages to walk up the stairs and into the blinding daylight. Once on the surface, there seemed to be no obvious way to enter Tiananmen Square, so I just followed the swarm, as they knew how the system worked, and we joined a slow moving mass of humanity. One line consisted of groups, and the other for couples, families, individuals and confused tourists. Away in the distance stood a barrier of blue canopies, marking the security check area. Even further ahead, a regular wave of visitors crossed the road and entered the square. 20 minutes later I finally arrived at the x-ray machine and dropped my backpack on the conveyer belt. Chinese nationals tapped their ID cards on an electronic pad, but being a GB passport holder, I was quickly waived through, as if my presence was a serious inconvenience. Based on what happened at Tiananmen Square in 1989, the enemy of the state was already inside her borders, and not a foreigner. Big Brother was watching us all.

While doing the tourist thing of shuffling about with my mouth open, I watched a young man in his late teens, sitting on the ground of Tiananmen Square. A policeman approached him, and I wondered if he would tell the youth to move in case someone tripped over him, but he just conducted a random ID card check. The officer walked away satisfied and continued to ask Chinese visitors for their identification. I wanted to follow this policeman, to see if he found any political dissidents, agitators or trouble-makers lurking in the crowd, but a noisy group of school kids in matching yellow T-shirts, separated us and he disappeared from sight. Many police and security officers stood around and patrolled the square. One immaculately uniformed officer stood under a small canopy to protect him from the sun, facing the crowd. He barely moved while scanning the crowd, stern faced.

141

Crossing the road from Tiananmen Square to the Forbidden Palace was easier than entering Tiananmen Square in the first place. However, the crowds grew thicker as the entrance grew closer.

The Meridian Gate, where Mao's portrait looks down at us, was a major disappointment. Close up, his image looked as if it was the world's largest paint-by-numbers work of art. Looking up at Mao were hundreds of impatient, hot visitors squeezing and pushing over the five bridges and through the main entrance. What would Mao make of today's China? He would be glad his country still followed the one-party rule, but horrified by how much capitalism had taken over. The thought that the State's beady eyes could be watching my every move took some of the shine off this world famous site. I wouldn't have been surprised to learn government officials used peepholes, in the eyes of Mao's portrait, to secretly watch the crowd below.

There's an old Chinese expression, "We can always fool a foreigner." There's also an old Glasgow expression "Oh, you bloody think so?" Anyway, there I was, minding my own business, acting like a tourist – a video of this, a photo of that – when two drop-dead gorgeous Chinese women appeared in my camera's viewfinder.

"Hello, do you speak English?" one asked. I immediately went on high alert due to the number of scams directed at single male Western visitors. Chinese women generally don't approach Western men, unless they are after one thing or another. "We would like to improve our English. Can we walk with you?"

Now, if this happened in Glasgow, I would have felt rather happy with myself, thanking God in all his glory, and basically everything. One woman seemed to be the boss, doing most of the talking. She looked immaculate, long dark hair, dark blue polo shirt, a black skirt above the knees and white tights (tights in +30°C temperatures?). Her partner in crime looked stunning, wearing a floral, rather tight fitting dress, also just above the knee, no tights, and with a figure, which I found difficult to ignore. Their grasp of English seemed pretty good to me, highlighting another scam alert.

"Can you speak Chinese?" she asked. As I answered "No.", they could now chat between themselves in Mandarin to formulate a cunning plan of action. The talkative one was named Jenny ("That's not my real name. My Chinese name would be too hard to pronounce."), and was quite touchy-feely. Her friend always walked ahead of us. Early into the encounter Jenny brought up the subject of the heat, and why a cool drink might be in order.

"You are from Scotland, so you like Scotch whisky?" Jenny asked. I told her no, and made the mistake of mentioning my love of the occasional lager.

I asked Jenny "Do you live here?"

"No, we are just here for the weekend. We are from Dalian. Have you heard of Dalian?"

"Yes" I said. "It's on the coast." Despite only visiting Beijing at weekends, they had a good knowledge of negotiating the Forbidden City. Jenny changed the subject.

Jenny complimented me about my shape. "Oh you run? You should run with Judy." she suggested, and Judy smiled. "You two have so much in common."

Jenny showed me a photo on her phone of her typical meal, a plate of vegetables. I missed the reason why she showed this to me, as the idea of Judy running in Lycra was still bouncing around in my head. Jenny suddenly announced she wanted a photo of us two lovebirds, Judy and myself, sitting side by side on the moat wall, and then came a good one, which had a ring of truth about it.

"You need to buy a ticket to get into the Forbidden City. You must buy them online, or buy on the day, but all tickets are now sold out. We have checked."

Visitor numbers to the Forbidden City were now limited to 'just' 80,000 per day (!) As annual visitor numbers had hit 16 million in 2017, the authorities decided to impose daily visitor limits to flatten out the peak days.

The point of this nugget of information was to emphasise I had no reason to hang around here, when I could be enjoying a cold beer with a couple of friendly Chinese girls. Jenny's routine continued, remarking how I looked in good shape and must take care of myself. If only she knew the truth. "Don't you wish you could walk around naked? Perhaps it is Judy that is making you hot? Bad joke. Sorry. Ha ha."

This scam was about flirting and getting your hopes up. Two

girls were better than one, increasing the odds the unsuspecting victim might have a preference. For a hot-blooded, heterosexual single male, this took a lot of self-control and Zen-like inner strength. I wished this scenario could have been different, but the logical half of the brain ruled. The girls take the unsuspecting tourist to a bar or tearoom, a pleasant hour is had by all until the bill comes, and surprise, surprise, you're taken to the cleaners. The prices were grossly inflated, and if you refused to pay, the heavies would come out and use their powers of persuasion to encourage compliance. In the meantime, your lovely lady friends have mysteriously disappeared, leaving you on your own.

We left the Forbidden City area and began to walk down a shady, adjacent street. We strolled through the local neighbourhood, and I felt rather happy for myself. Locals looked at me and probably thought "There goes another foreigner fooled by the Chinese". However I resisted the temptation of following the girls into a quiet, narrow alleyway, and instead stayed on the busier roads. I have a good memory for maps, so knew where we were heading, although I couldn't tell you what I had for breakfast this morning.

Their aim was to relieve me of my cash supply. My scam was to waste their time, denying the girls an opportunity to earn an income from me, or anyone else, for at least an hour.

After ten minutes they found an attractive open-air bar which they said looked welcoming. As we had passed several similar-looking bars already, I realised this was their preferred crime scene. While Jenny kept me occupied outside, Judy disappeared inside, probably saying something like "Hey Zhang Wei. We've got another pigeon outside. Get the table ready."

Jenny began to walk into the bar, and I just stood there on the pavement. She looked back at me, surprised. I said, "Look, I'm hot and beginning to struggle. I'm just heading back to my hotel to relax."

The look on her face was one of disbelief. "You could have told us earlier!" She turned on her heels, flipped her hair, and marched inside. Fortunately the head on my shoulders ruled, and the afternoon ended up as a happy memory instead of a bad one.

Now the girls would waste valuable time, lining up, working their way through security again and battle the crowds back to the

Forbidden Palace. Ain't I a stinker?

For centuries travellers have commented on the Chinese love of hocking and spitting. To begin with, there is an ear-shattering hock, which announces to all, that the person in question was about to expurgate. The spitting part was equally gross. Some spat the results of the hock into the nearest bush or against a tree while several spat in front of them, and others spat to their sides. Chinese all walk at the same slow speed, and as a fast-walker, I continually overtook slower walkers. It would only be a matter of time before a splatter would land on my ankle. Jenny and Judy didn't hock, as that might have been bad for attracting business. Old women produced the loudest hocks, and I secretly hoped this delightful habit would die out once the older population died out too. Some men hocked and spat, and stood on the results, as if grinding the blob into the ground like you would treat a cigarette butt. I couldn't imagine anything else, which could be added to this, to make the spitting event more disgusting.

Today had been hot and humid, and even the locals struggled with the oppressive stickiness. Beads of sweat constantly ran down the side of Jenny's face, which she never wiped away. Perhaps this was part of the visual 'Look how hot it is. Let's grab a cool drink.' ploy.

Shoppers wiped their faces and fanned themselves, their shirts soaked in sweat. By 4pm the sky had changed colour from a light grey to slate grey, and huge drops began to splat on the roads and pavements. Summertime downpours were a part of daily life in Beijing. Locals knew the signs and they quickly made a move for doorways for protection. I just slapped a hat on my head and kept walking, being already soaked to the skin with sweat. The cooler rainwater would be a great relief as I walked to the nearest Metro station.

All Metro trains had at least one security guard. The guard I saw today, perhaps in his early 20s, wore a misfitting uniform. His light blue shirt was two sizes too large, which hung off his body. His dark blue, baggy trousers were tailored for a man closer to six feet in height. The cuffs dragged on the floor. It seemed a shame an organisation the size of the Beijing Metro couldn't give this man a uniform, which would fit a little better. China may have a 'one country two systems' style of government, but a 'one size fits all' system for staff uniforms.

Another 'must do' while in Beijing involved a visit to the Great Wall of China. The nearest point to which the wall passed Beijing was at a place called Badaling. Guidebooks and even a man at the hotel front desk all advised against a weekend visit. My 'Russian Revenge' showed signs of flaring up again, so decided not to make the trip today. I faced the potential of a long, uncomfortable day without a western style toilet, and using a squat-style toilet would be an unpleasant experience, not just for me, but for others around me.

At night, feeling brave, I walked to nearby Qianmen Street and I couldn't have been more disappointed. The crowds, noise and the sight of a 'Ripley's Believe it or Not' museum, made me realise this area would be well below my retail expectations. I spotted a parallel street further down a couple of alleys heading off to the right. A few shoppers strolled about, so decided to return back along that way instead of Qianmen Street.

This narrow, parallel street, called Liangshidian, was more like it – small noodle shops, randomly parked scooters, no tourists and no tourist tat. As my 'Putin's Panos' was making itself known again, I reluctantly headed back to my hotel determined to eat at Liangshidian Street tomorrow, belly permitting.

In busy areas of Beijing, small electric police cars and mobile police stations strategically sat at street corners, guarded by bored police officers. These vehicles would sit there, flashing their red and blue lights, serving as a visual reminder to behave and not to forget Big Brother was watching us all. Security cameras were pointing in all directions, and if there ever was a police state, I was standing in it. From around 2000, China has seen a steady increase in public disorder and murmurings against the State. To combat this growing trend, China embraced technology, and if it's recent record of human rights is anything to go by, it is now winning the battle.

Back at the hotel, I decided to eat at the hotel's restaurant. The idea of Nasi Goreng appealed to me, so imagine my disappointment when the smiling waiter advised "Nasi Goring is off menu". As the meals were made from scratch, what could the problem be? No rice? Eggs gone off? I settled for a chicken curry, which, in all honesty, was extremely tasty, and spicy enough to make my nose run.

DAY 26:
GREAT WALL OF CHINA

I was determined to visit the Great Wall of China, but not as part of an organised tour. These excursions were non-refundable, and in the wet season, a dry day could never be guaranteed. Typhoon season meant the possibility of heavy rain and strong winds. There would be little shelter on the Great Wall, resulting in a very wet and miserable day indeed. When in Beijing, do as the Beijingers do – catch a local train on the day, if the weather forecast suggested a dry day ahead.

Online reviews gave many reasons why Badaling should be avoided, primarily due to the crowds. Even the girl at my hotel front desk advised "Badaling is not good." What's better than a bit of culture shock and a challenge in a country where you don't speak the language?

Local suburban trains ran to Badaling. Weekends and holidays were apparently a nightmare due to the huge crowds, and since I disliked crowds ("Why the hell did you travel to China then?" I hear you ask.), timing was important. Today was neither a weekend or a holiday, so I bit the bullet and decided to travel to Badaling and see the Great Wall of China.

Despite being at the end of morning rush hour, the Metro train to Huangtudian station wasn't too crowded. So far so good. My first true challenge would be to find my way from Huoying Metro station to Huangtudian S2 surface station. I wasn't sure which way I should head, due to a lack of English language signs, so just followed the locals, because they knew where to go.

At Huangtudian, passengers were corralled into two waiting areas. Despite the signage on walls, instructions on the platforms and through loudspeaker announcements, ordering the crowd not to run, when the gates eventually opened, allowing us onto the platform, the crowd ran.

A mass of several hundred hot, excited and impatient passengers stampeded through the doors, onto the platform, and fanned out in both directions towards the train doors. Being British, running for a seat is not the done thing. Instead, I walked briskly and with purpose, as standing for 1½ hours didn't appeal to me. By heading straight towards the rear of the train, I found a corner seat by a window, made myself comfortable, and prepared myself for what lay ahead.

Announcements on Beijing Metro TV systems remind passengers of the importance of upholding Chinese traditions, such as offering your seat to the infirm or elderly, and taking care of children. The Chinese tradition of pushing and shoving did not require a reminder, as this habit seemed to be endemic. Back in the UK, if someone pushed me from behind in a crowd, my automatic reaction would be to actually slow down or even worse to accidentally step backwards onto a toe or two.

Perhaps the frustration at the lack of space encouraged pushing, and the only way to negotiate a bottleneck of humanity was to shove those in front of you. Not so. Yesterday I stood on a Metro station platform, and waited for the incoming train to stop, and the automatic doors to open. Door areas are clearly marked on the platform, and commuters are continually reminded to stand aside and let passengers off first. Ignore this simple instruction and a Metro employee will bark at you to clear the area. I saw no other passenger waiting to board at this door, so stood to the left and waited for the doors to open. I then sensed someone standing behind me. When the doors opened, he pushed and squeezed between me and the side of the train, to be the first on board, and then proceeded to stand by the door. I fought the temptation to accidentally stand on a few toes as I passed him.

Travel author Paul Theroux summed the need to push in his 2000 book 'Fresh-Air Fiend' - "Whenever a signal is given in China, people jump. It is as though there is a deep racial memory of individuals having gone hungry or got lost or left behind because they hesitated or weren't aggressive enough. Learned from periods of poverty, the habit has now become a Chinese reflex, the instinct to push towards any door, any vehicle, any ticket window; shoving is the only way forward."

Back to my Badaling adventure. The carriage had now filled, and a few slower, unfortunate travellers faced a ninety-minute journey on their feet. Through the carriage, the sense of station panic and chaos subsided. Our train glided out of the station, and passed through the ugly urbanisation of northern Beijing, followed by fields criss-crossed by electricity pylons. No view of rural China seemed to be complete without pylons.

About 30 minutes into the journey, the first hills appeared, and soon our train slowed to negotiate a 3.3% gradient. This line had an unusual zigzag, or switchback. I hadn't realised this until now (to be honest it had never even crossed my mind), but zigzags tended to be single-track lines. The line to Badaling was double-track, and on this line the tracks diverged and had their own zigzag. Badaling-bound trains reversed on the western switchback and the Beijing-bound trains reversed on the eastern switchback.

Fifteen minutes before our scheduled arrival in Badaling, the noise level increased when passengers on the left side of the train glimpsed their first view of the Great Wall of China. Considering the fine views available at Badaling, this didn't stop passengers from attempting to photograph the wall. All they would achieve would be a poor image, revealing a reflection of their excited faces in the window, and the green blur of passing trees and bushes. Sitting on the right side of the train, I could only catch glimpses of the wall, snaking up a ridge. Most passengers on my side eventually decided to stand up for a better look out of the left-hand windows, blocking my view entirely.

Badaling was an easy day trip from Beijing, so why did we have so many excited people, of all ages, on board? Surely most had seen the wall before?

Leaving the train at Badaling was much more orderly compared to the embarkation at Huangtudian, with no pushing, shoving or running.

Around 700 passengers spilled onto the platform and proceeded to stroll at half speed towards the station exit. Chinese people can walk quickly, but only when it suited them, otherwise they just seemed to shuffle along.

Due to the Badaling horror stories, I decided on a plan of action in advance, by avoiding the main entrance and heading for the cable car. This cunning plan would carry me to the highest point in the area, and from there I would walk back down to the shops, offices, bus and car parks and the general chaos. Unfortunately I couldn't find a kiosk or counter to buy a cable car ticket. Many shops sold tickets for the lower wall access, but finding tickets for the cable car had become more of a challenge.

My first enquiry at a ticket window resulted in a vague look of disbelief, as if my query had been for a hot air balloon ride. My second request, at another kiosk, resulted in a helpful girl pointing towards the entrance building, where several hundred visitors formed a long, snaking line, many under umbrellas for shade. Surely they didn't share the same idea as me, did they?

Time for Plan B. Tour guides often know a limited amount of English, so I approached one thinking, "Third time lucky". The tour guide smiled and pointed to a rather large Chinese language sign featuring a QR code. She said, to ride the cable car I must scan the QR code, and through my WeChat account, apply for an e-ticket. I didn't have a Chinese WeChat account, so my plan was completely scuppered. No wonder I couldn't understand the system or lack of tickets for sale.

I walked disgruntled back to the main entrance gate, and joined the shuffling crowd, which had now arrived *en masse* from the train station. The wall was busy, but not the feared shoulder-to-shoulder mass of humanity. Crowds were thickest at the towers, where visitors escaped the blazing sun by standing inside the signal towers, in the shade and coolness. This created bottlenecks at regular intervals, in particular at the entrance and exits. No one seemed to have the spatial awareness to realise, by standing in a four-foot wide passage, forcing people to push past, this was perhaps not a good place to stand. Perhaps the Government's Chinese traditions advertising campaign should, in future, include this oversight.

There's an urban myth that the Great Wall is the only manmade structure visible from space. This story began 30 years before the first human went into orbit. It can be seen, but not by the naked eye. At around 5 metres or 16 feet in width, you've got a better chance of seeing your local street, railway line, airport runway, town or city than the Great Wall. Because the wall follows natural contours and colours of the landscape, it blends in pretty well. I imagine, much to the disappointment of the Chinese Government's propaganda department, China's first astronaut, Yang Liwei, went into space in 2003 and

150

reported the wall couldn't be seen out his capsule window.

Some sections of wall date from 1505, and all sections include numerous flights of steps, continually up and down, up and down. That's what happens when you build a defensive wall on a ridge top, and why many refer to the wall as the Stone Dragon. The many small sloping areas, without steps, had seen their stonework worn away in places to an inch lower than the surrounding mortar, which seemed to stand the test of time better. How long would the wall survive this current rate of footstep erosion?

I later read in a state media report around 30% of this UNESCO World Heritage site had disappeared due to natural erosion, damage from tourists and the stealing of bricks for homes. ("Hey Li Qiang, I like your new driveway. Where did you get those antique looking stones from?") Now I understood why the passengers on my train to Badaling had been so excited. It was sheer relief to see the wall still standing.

Overall, the visit to Badaling was a positive and thoroughly enjoyable experience, and I gained a real feeling of satisfaction in fighting the odds and crowds. Some of the best experiences occur when you leave your comfort zone.

Back in Beijing, electric motor bikes struck a chord with me. I couldn't see (or more accurately hear) any petrol powered motor bikes. Not a single one. The Government's attempt to control the city's notorious smog problem seemed well under way. To be honest, during my stay in the city, I didn't become aware of a smog issue, so perhaps the Government was winning the battle.

Riding an electric motor bike appealed to me, but living on the second floor of a 1900-built apartment building would make recharging slightly tricky. Another drawback would be Glasgow's 'moist maritime' climate, where rain is registered five days out of seven. Regular exposure to the elements on an electric bike might not be such an enjoyable experience.

Another hurdle in the adoption of the Chinese electric bike scheme back home would be the habit of riding on pavements. I tended not to walk on Beijing's roads, and so motorcyclists not riding on my pavement, I thought, was a good compromise. Often, when walking along a pavement, absorbing the smells, sights and sounds of Beijing, an electric motor bike rider would quietly approach from behind. The rider would honk his horn, suggesting in the Chinese tradition I step off my pavement and let him past. In the Glaswegian tradition, I would totally ignore him and keep walking, because he shouldn't be there in the first place.

Direction and information signs seemed to confuse some locals. My excuse was I couldn't read Chinese, but it wasn't just me. Whether navigating the Great Wall of China entrance at Badaling, negotiating Metro stations, or wandering through shopping centres, locals seem to be confused on a regular basis. They would continually stop to look around, change direction without warning, or ask for directions. Was there something inherently wrong with Chinese language signage? Here in the UK, Network Rail uses a particular font in all railway signage, which research has shown is interpreted by the brain quickest. Road signs also use a particular font due to its visual clarity from a distance. However, it was common for Chinese to stop and stare at a sign as if they couldn't comprehend what it said.

The Chinese language doesn't use an alphabet, but sets of characters, which form pictures, and many characters look similar. To speak comfortably you need to know 500-750 characters and to read a newspaper around 2,000 characters. The Great Compendium of Chinese Characters says there are 54,648 characters and The Dictionary of Chinese Variant Form claims there are 106,230. Unless you are an academic or well educated, perhaps it takes a second or two longer to fully absorb a sign, and hence a delay and the need to suddenly stop in your tracks.

Here's a controversial comment warning: Although most Chinese women dress smart and conservatively, a small number looked as if they had dressed themselves in the dark. I appreciate Glasgow isn't the catwalk capital of Europe, but the confusing combination of clothes often left me staring in bewilderment. All I can say is a few Chinese fashions were unique, and they wouldn't work anywhere else but in China.

I noticed a trend for English language slogans on shirts. These words of wisdom often made no sense, as if an error had been made during translation through an online (Government approved) translator.

I saw a few T-shirts, which featured random letters on the front, which looked intriguing and 'foreign' in their eyes, but in reality made no sense at all. I spotted two women, both in their 20s, wearing T-shirts which proudly announced "Be At Wave" and the other "Start To Stop Clapping." Say what?

In a silly Monty Python inspired moment I thought about releasing a range of English language T-shirts here in China, displaying the caption 'My Hovercraft Is Full Of Eels.' emblazoned on the front. If you are familiar with the sketch, you might understand the joke.

After sunset I returned to Liangshidian Street which I stumbled upon last night. Occasional drops of rain were becoming more numerous, so this was taken as a sign to quickly find a restaurant. Most shops lacked a front wall, and being open to the fresh air, this allowed me to look in and case each joint before entering, without making a total touristic fool of myself.

After sitting down at a table, a girl handed me a colourful menu, in Chinese and English. She left me alone for a few moments so I could contemplate the menu, eventually deciding on the deep fried pork strips, and also pork and scallion dumplings. The unfazed girl serving me, unfazed as she wasn't worried about a language barrier getting in the way, opened up an app on her phone and through state-approved translating software, scanned the description and showed me, in English, the contents of the dumplings. The meal was washed down with a Yanjing beer, brewed here in Beijing. As I worked my way through this banquet, the rain outside became a downpour. The narrow street became a torrent of running water, causing people to skip through the puddles looking for shelter. I was dry, eating an excellent meal and enjoying a local brew. I was a happy man.

By the time I finished my meal, paid the bill (78 Yuan = £8.80), and burped quietly, the heavy rain had stopped, so waddled back in the general direction of my hotel. The air was warm, the cicadas began to chirp again, and even the constant stream of rickshaw drivers calling out "Hello!" and "Where are you going?" couldn't burst my happy bubble.

DAY 27:
BEIJING TO SHANGHAI

Having completed a trial run of the Metro connection to Beijing South station already, I checked out of my hotel full of confidence. I felt relaxed and actually enjoyed the ride, despite being part of the rush hour crush. Unlike my earlier trial run to Beijing South, the interior of this train was shoulder-to-shoulder humanity.

Beijing South Station was massive, but easy to navigate, helped by an absence of pushing and shoving. Perhaps the allocated seat numbers on high-speed trains alleviated this problem. The main station board listed 36 train departures and 36 arrivals, and this was for just the next hour.

Once on the platform I wandered up to the front of this futuristic, sleek high-speed train to grab a photo of this engineering marvel, but the length of the train was exactly the same length as the platform. At the extreme end of the platform, where signs clearly indicated where I shouldn't stand I thought, "What harm will one photo cause?" I found out. On an adjacent platform sat a uniformed man, parked on a small stool, holding a megaphone. He patiently watched me, and once my optimum photographic spot had been determined, he barked at me through his megaphone to leave the area. I don't understand Mandarin, but fully understood his instruction, so obeyed it without question, but not before taking my photo.

My high-speed train to Shanghai left on time and soon reached a maximum speed of 350 kilometres per hour (217mph) once we left central Beijing. After a short while, a uniformed woman began to sweep the aisle of the train. The ride was super smooth, so I decided to carry out a simple experiment on the window frame. Would a small upside down bottle of water and a 2 Euro coin, standing on its edge, stay upright? You bet. At 350 kilometres per hour, there was barely a ripple on the water in my clear plastic bottle, and the 2 Euro coin stood perfectly still.

Sitting to my right was a man in his early 20s, named Joucim. I

154

didn't recognise where he was from, but mentioned his town was near Barcelona. He had been watching S.H.I.E.L.D. on his phone until my window ledge experiment distracted his attention. By the time the second episode had started, he was asleep.

South of Beijing, ugly urban sprawl dominated the landscape, with high-rise apartment buildings a permanent feature in the hazy distance. Construction cranes poked into the sky, concrete railway viaducts and roads criss-crossed the landscape, broken only by the occasional green river and foul looking stagnant pond. And of course, the scene wouldn't be perfect without lines of electricity pylons disappearing into the hazy distance. No part of the scenery avoided human manipulation of some sort.

Although the rapid development of China was nothing short of impressive, I worried about the amount of concrete used. Not only did China manufacture and use around 60% of the world's cement, but cement production creates a major source of atmospheric carbon dioxide.

Many concrete constructions in the West have been found to last only 50 or 60 years before problems develop, with some only surviving a few years before issues were discovered. Should the Chinese economy cool down, would the country be able to afford the maintenance and replacement costs of these thousands of concrete buildings and viaducts?

Unannounced, we began to cross the impressive 114 kilometre, or 70.8 mile long, Langfang–Qingxian viaduct, the second longest bridge in the world. While crossing the viaduct, all passengers in our carriage received a complimentary bottle of water or cola and a colourful gift box containing a small cake and a fruit based chewy sweet.

The handouts were followed by a succession of staff selling A4 size books in the Chinese language with traditional vertical text, model trains and hot meals. An hour later the girls attempted to sell the leftover hot meals, followed by drinks, fruit, model trains and more fruit. The girls used an airline-style trolley to move the produce along the aisle, with plastic tubs displaying a myriad of fruity colours.

Two hours into our journey we passed through hills and the

train slid through our first high-speed tunnel. Construction sites dotted the landscape. High-speed rail viaducts sat unused, waiting for their overhead wires to be installed and a dual-carriageway road lay void of traffic. Only the occasional truck carting away spoil created any movement. Dozens of identical, bland, ugly high-rise apartments sat without occupants. Where would the population come from to fill these horrible high-rise buildings? If the Government provided for a mass influx of people from rural China into urban areas, would there be enough left in the countryside to manage it? Due to the One Child policy, in operation from 1979 until 2016, there were barely enough children born to replace the adult numbers. In fact, China's population growth was one of the world's lowest, at only 0.6% per year. If the population wasn't growing sufficiently to justify the urban sprawl, were these new urbanites arriving from rural areas?

After we crossed the Yangtze River, the train made a brief stop at Nanjing, before continuing to Shanghai. What was impressive about this portion of the journey was the viaduct our train sped along. The Danyang–Kunshan Grand Bridge probably doesn't mean much to most, but this was the longest bridge in the world, at an incredible 169 kilometres or 105 miles in length, at an average height of 100 metres or 328 feet above the ground. One stretch of the bridge crossed the Yangcheng Lake, 9 kilometres or 5.6 miles wide. It was an incredible engineering feat.

As canals, rivers and lakes criss-crossed the land, an extremely long viaduct, which avoided the wetland below, was the most efficient solution. A viaduct would also prevent livestock and the occasional farmer from wandering across the tracks.

SHANGHAI, CHINA

I had booked an attractive rate at a 4-star property near the Bund, which offered a river view of the Suzhou River, a tributary of the wider Huangpu River. As a result, The Bund Riverside name was geographyically correct, being just 400 metres from the Bund, and by the side of a river, but not the river everyone imagined when thinking of Shanghai.

I had booked a superior queen room with a river view. The man at the check-in desk tapped his keyboard and peered into his monitor as if trying to rectify a problem. I wish hotel check-in clerks wouldn't do that. Had I booked the wrong dates, presented myself at the wrong hotel, was the room double-booked or even no reservation?

He frowned and eventually said he could only offer me a low floor only and this wouldn't have a great view, although I could upgrade to a superior grade room if I wished. A good try, but having worked in retail sales all of my life, I was aware of this up-selling technique, and this trick didn't work with me.

"The room you have for me will be fine." I said. He continued to tap away on his keyboard. "I can offer an 'Executive Double' on the 16th floor at no extra cost."

Now he was talking. The 'Executive Room' was called 'executive' because a desk and chair were included in the price, and not much else. However, the highlight of the room was outside the window - the spectacular view, far superior to the splendid view of the Warsaw skyline from the Novotel. At night the view of the commercial centre of Shanghai, and its unique, modern architecture, quickly became the highlight of the trip so far. Unfortunately Executive Rooms at the Bund Riverside Hotel did not include complimentary slippers.

Today had been a long day, so I lay down for 5 minutes and woke 5 hours later.

DAY 28:
SHANGHAI, CHINA

After a lazy day of sightseeing, I decided on a relaxing evening walk to the Bund, on the bank of the Huangpu River, but had never seen such crowds in all of my life. Roads were strictly controlled, with crowds heading to the Bund on the street's right side pavement and returning crowds on the left. Step off the pavement and onto the road and you will be barked at by a stern faced police officer through a megaphone, advising your lack of understanding was not in the Chinese tradition and you must step back in line. Individuals not following the rules would not be tolerated. I made the mistake of walking against the tide of humanity at one point, and although not shouted at, I soon realised I was the odd one out. Going against the flow was not permitted in China, so I quickly crossed the road and followed the rules before any police officers shouted at me, and became one of the obedient masses.

A huge crowd surged towards the Bund tonight. I wondered whether a special event, such as a fireworks display or light show, was the attraction. My only experience of this size of crowd had been at football grounds, when the swarm of bodies all left at the same time after the match. There must have been a crowd in excess of 100,000 visiting the river tonight. With a population of over 24 million, perhaps the numbers weren't all that large for Shanghai.

Chen Yi Square, on the Bund side of the river, offered the best views of the unique skyline. I stood with my mouth open, staring at the cityscape of Shanghai's futuristic commercial area of light, from a crowd of seven or eight deep. Out of nowhere a Chinese woman began talking to me. Now, I don't usually have attractive women initiating conversations with me. Come to think of it, I don't have the unattractive ones doing that either. Immediately my brain clicked into 'alert' mode for a scam.

Her name was Lynn, and she was learning how to cook.

"I am specialising in dim sims and steamed buns".

I told her I loved steamed buns. She had returned from Japan just three days earlier after learning the Japanese techniques. Talking to her about food was fabulous, but in the back of my mind a question niggled away. Was she genuinely chatty, or was there an ulterior motive? After a while it began.

"You like Chinese beer? Let's go for a drink."

"I don't drink beer before bed because I'll be heading to my hotel soon and I have an early rise tomorrow morning."

"Where are you travelling to?"

"Nanning."

"Why are you going to Nanning?" she asked, with a confused look on her face.

"A train goes there. I'm travelling to Hanoi in Vietnam, and Nanning is in the way." Lynn nodded. "I must change trains there and stay overnight, so I'll look at the sights."

"There's not much to see there." She immediately steered the conversation back to drinking.

"You don't have to go to a bar on Nanjing Road. Where are you staying?" (alarm bells ringing loudly).

"The Bund Riverside" I said.

"Oh, nice hotel. They have a jazz bar there."

"Oh really?" I thought, imagining the narrow bar and how it would struggle to hold a dozen people.

I reluctantly bid Lynn farewell. She had been great fun to talk to, spoke excellent English, and had been a window to a confusing culture. I just wish there hadn't been the nagging feeling a scam was in progress.

I walked, as part of the obedient throng, back to Nanjing Road to look for somewhere to eat which wasn't packed.

"Hello. Where are you from?" asked a petite Chinese woman. I went through the same responses as with Lynn, and this time the alarm bells rang loud and clear. Our conversation didn't extend to exchanging names, and I avoided any detailed conversation. And then it began.

"You fancy a beer?"

"No thanks."

"How about a coffee?" I politely bid her farewell, and another Chinese woman replaced her.

"Hello mister. Where are you from?"

This woman seemed genuinely surprised I didn't want to get to know her. If she ever visits Glasgow, then maybe, possibly definitely, but on her home turf, definitely not.

Three women in twenty minutes - a personal best. Unlike the Beijing daytime scam, where the girls take their victims to a pre-arranged tearoom and reduce the weight of their wallets, this scam took place in the shopping heart of Shanghai on a busy night, a beer or coffee, your place or mine. Their conversations all followed the same pattern. The situation stunk of a scam, but I couldn't work out what it could be. Girl number two began making a phone call as we shuffled along Nanjing Road, so I wondered if she was arranging a rendezvous with an accomplice.

On the front desk of the Bund Riverside Hotel sat a sign in several languages offering useful tips. One stated "Don't follow strangers into the bar." I guessed this referred to the hotel's 'jazz' bar, which Lynn mentioned. Could a scam be in operation, even at a 4-star hotel? Hotel management couldn't stop a foreign guest from drinking in the bar with a local, but the reception desk still displayed a warning sign, so there must have been a reason.

These girls were dressed in the usual conservative Chinese way and didn't come over as prostitutes. They just didn't seem to look or act like… ehem… tarts. Even Jenny and Judy were dressed to attract the attention, and keep the attention, of a single male. For one moment it crossed my mind to possibly go with the flow to discover the scam, but I didn't fancy the possible financial damage if things made a turn for the worst. After all, I prefer a happy ending. I even asked the girl at reception on checkout about a possible scam, but she denied all knowledge.

I later brought this subject up with two Chinese students on the overnight Nanning-Hanoi train. We shared the same compartment, and they spoke good English. According to one of the girls, this wasn't a scam! She explained the Chinese see Caucasians on TV and in movies. In Beijing foreigners were not uncommon, but by travelling towards Shanghai and further south, foreigners became fewer and further between. Being a solo traveller, I was fair game. Some ladies actually found me interesting. (I've never said that before). This would be good for their street cred to be seen having drinks with a foreigner, just like my street cred in Glasgow would be embellished if I was spotted having drinks with an exotic woman (or, come to think of it, any woman).

I read on social media these girls were indeed prostitutes, but I still had my doubts. This seemed to be a prolonged, roundabout way of getting to the point. Time is money after all. Women in that profession made their intentions clear with the suggestion of a massage, or gave 'the look' as you approached them. Perhaps the local technique was to have a few drinks, relax, drop any inhibitions, and after building up a good rapport, one thing would lead to another and the possibility of a financial transaction. The process just seemed to be too drawn-out.

I was attracting the girls like bees to honey (Hey, I've never said that before either), so decided to avoid Nanjing Road and the attention of the ladies. I found sanctuary in a large, multistorey shopping complex, full of fashion shops and no where to eat. My meal plan fell flat and so reluctantly went to the other extreme – Chinese noodles from the supermarket in the shopping centre. How disappointing.

I enjoyed my stay in Shanghai, and would love to return one day. Unlike Beijing, Shanghai had more character, a little more gritty in places, not so modern or government focussed. The ladies found me more interesting as well.

DAY 29:
SHANGHAI TO NANNING

I quickly realised few passengers on my train would be travelling all of the way to Nanning. Only foolish tourists would be crazy enough to complete such a long trip, even by high-speed train, when a visitor could fly in a fraction of the time. The majority of Chinese still used cheaper long-distance buses, but high-speed train services were slowly cutting into that market. Despite described as a high-speed service, this train operated as a 'short hop' or semi-local service. Passengers arrived and left at each station.

My first companion was a well-dressed woman in her 30s who spent most of her time chattering on her phone. She lasted one stop, to be replaced by a man of around 25 who would yawn loudly, nap or use his phone.

In front of me sat a man in his late 30s, bald and of a stocky build. He wore a dark blue vest, or 'wife beater', and a thick gold chain around his neck. He wanted to look 'tough', but his small frame prevented him from being taken seriously, at least in my eyes. Mister Toughguy used his phone to watch a TV show, and without giving any consideration towards his fellow travellers, insisted on full volume. His attitude and air of cockiness suggested he did not actually give one single, solitary fuck. Keeping volume under control was not, as I understand, one of the traditional Chinese traditions to be upheld.

I wasn't the only passenger annoyed by his excessive noise. A woman one row behind me stood up to find the culprit, and my colleague asked him to turn the volume down. The volume fluctuated in an act of defiance and when he finally turned off his phone, he fell asleep, giving us peace.

Chinese people seemed to tolerate noise more than the British. By living in such crowded and close quarters, they were possibly unaware of the noise they made. As an individual, your noise was drowned out by those around you. Perhaps the British were a quieter race, although if you could hear my neighbours, you might not agree

162

with me.

When we stopped at Nanchang station, and the train became quieter, I could hear at least five separate phones on loud speaker in the carriage. I guessed the use of earphones, or using a phone normally, by actually holding it to your ear, was one area of technology not exploited by China yet, and therefore exempt from the importance of upholding Chinese traditions. On two occasions a train supervisor asked passengers to turn their phone volumes down.

At one point I feared the man to my left had pissed himself, but soon realised the smell originated from his fishy, shrimp snack he was munching. After he popped the last piece of light grey flesh into his mouth, the smell lingered on his breath. Whenever he yawned, the smell intensified. He left the train at Heng Yangdong, around halfway between Shanghai and Nanning, to be immediately replaced by a man in his 30s who snorted occasionally and kept himself amused fiddling with his mobile phone. Perhaps he was determining how the hands-free facility worked.

Many Chinese passengers preferred to shout when on a call. A couple of passengers bellowed so loudly on their calls, I wondered whether using a phone was actually necessary.

Phone man left at Qiyang and stop by stop, the train began to empty. The wannabe Triad in front of me left at Youzhou, along with several others, leaving the train less than half full, and also much quieter.

I saw my first rice paddy near Henyang, and realised the landscape fell into two categories between Beijing and Nanning – mountainous or dead flat. There seemed to be no regions of gently undulating hills – only one extreme or the other.

Near Xingan I purchased a Chinese Railways meal, which the sales girl described as "Vegetables!". I was impressed she knew this difficult word, since few adults I met could speak any English, other than in hotels and the occasional 'over-friendly' girl on the street. I wasn't hungry, but curious to see what the meal composed of. My vegetarian meal consisted of shredded carrot, cubes of tofu, cabbage and a generous helping of sticky rice. It was difficult for visitors to go hungry in China unless they relied on knives and forks. Western cutlery was close to non-existent outside of hotel and airport restaurants. The Chinese are a clever race. They invented papermaking, the compass, gunpowder, and printing, so why could they not invent eating implements more practical than chopsticks.

Chopsticks became a table utensil around 400-500 AD. At that time China experienced a population boom and cooking resouces became scarce. Food cut into smaller pieces cooked faster, rendering the need for table knives obsolete. Chopsticks, which had been used for cooking, gradually became used for eating. They were also cheap and easily made.

At Guilin the train experienced a mass exodus of passengers, including any tourists, who came here to see the spectacular karst topography. As per usual, I was the exception, continuing onto Nanning.

NANNING, CHINA

Our train slid into the sleek and modern Nanning East station on time. I negotiated the Metro system seamlessly and in just 20 minutes I found myself in Central Nanning. On board the Metro train, many people glanced in my direction, and I would later learn a single westerner in Nanning was a rare sight. This was a little unnerving as I have always hated being centre of attention.

Nanning appeared much more bustling and disorganised than Shanghai, which, in turn, was more disorganised than Beijing. The further I travelled from the capital, the more noisier and grittier China became.

Electric bikes also ruled the roads here in Nanning. They zipped around in groups and dominated the pedestrian crossings and pavements. Before electric bikes became the norm, Chinese cities, full of farting, smog producing petrol fuelled motorbikes must have been a vision of Hell in summer. The reduction in air pollution, by adopting electric bikes, was balanced out by an increase in noise pollution due to the incessant honking of horns. "I'm overtaking." Honk. "I'm being overtaken." Honk. "It's my birthday today!" Honk. "I'd better check my horn is still working." Honk.

DAY 30:
NANNING, CHINA

Few tourists ventured as south as Nanning. Locals, young and old, would stare at me, possibly mesmerised by my large Caucasian nose. They saw western culture on TV and in the films, but to see one in real life - Wow!

I visited the picturesque People's Park and sat in the shade of a tree, watching a dozen women dancing in choreographic slow motion to the blare of Chinese music. I then noticed movement in my peripheral vision. A woman gestured to her two sons to stand behind me. She was preparing to take a stealth photo of me with her boys in the background! She had been caught red handed, and only then did she gesture if she could take a photo. I indicated a photo was okay, and with one boy on either side, I became the centre of attention and also guessed the highlight of their day. What a bizarre experience. I wondered what would happen, back home, if I asked my son to stand behind a Pakistani man so a stealth photo could be taken?

While wandering around this beautiful park, a security officer in a black uniform, with the Chinese flag stitched onto his right shoulder, caught my eye. He made a detour and walked towards six women who sat on a colourful blanket in the shade of a large tree. After a few questions, the officer photographed each picnicker with his mobile phone. I once read Big Brother frowned upon groups of people, and by snapping each individual's photo, it would act as an incentive not to deviate from the Party line, as you were now officially on record.

The Chinese Government objected to 'planned or impromptu gatherings that form because of internal contradiction'. Despite some research, I wasn't able to determine how large a gathering could be before a group became a concern to the police. In all fairness, it was possible these ladies were hatching a plot to overthrow the central Chinese Government, planning to assassinate a leading Chinese politician, or more likely just enjoying a catch-up with friends away from the incessant noise of downtown Nanning.

The number one priority, while in Nanning, was a visit to the night market. My plan of action was to try as many different foods as possible. I thought only tourists ate the deep fried crickets and scorpions, but locals were munching into these delicacies as well, so decided to give both a try.

The crickets and the scorpion were tasteless other than an underlying hint of charcoal and relieved to see the man serving me remembered to snip off the stinger at the tip of the scorpion's tail. This little piece of detail had actually crossed my mind. What would happen if he had been distracted while serving me, and ended up with more than I bargained for. Would scorpion poisoning by ingestion be covered by my travel insurance? The scorpion was skewered and liberally brushed with a pink, spicy sauce. Although happy to try new foods, I drew a line with centipedes, and especially the seafood, which wasn't worth the risk in a Chinese open-air market.

A student approached me and explained he wanted to practice his pronunciation. After two questions he disappeared into the crowd to join his friends, probably a little nervous or unsure about speaking to a gweilo.

If I hadn't been on my own, it's unlikely he would have approached me. Someone once asked if I ever felt lonely when travelling on my own. Travelling solo guarantees more interactions with locals and therefore more memories. Although there are advantages of travelling with someone, when it comes to interactions, I believe your experiences are diluted and softened by the reassurance of another person by your side. You are less likely to be approached or spoken to by strangers. Travelling with someone means you always have someone to talk to. Travelling solo means you must try a little harder and you must be prepared to expect the unexpected.

The evening air felt stifling, exasperated by the crowded stalls on either side of the narrow street, each with pots of boiling oil, sizzling grills and bright lights. Although 'Food Street' had been a culinary experience never to be forgotten, I had no desire to linger, as the heat had become unbearable.

DAY 31:
NANNING TO HANOI

I sat in the waiting area outside Nanning station, to conduct a little people watching before boarding my train. After ten minutes the young woman to my right, in her early 20s, indicated she wanted to take a photo of her and me. I consented, and I soon appeared on WeChat. The matter wasn't given any more thought until I caught her also taking a stealth video of me. I wagged my finger at her in mock disapproval, and we both laughed. I later caught her manipulating the video using a state approved filter app. I now wore lipstick (fire engine red – not my colour) and make-up! She was given a light-hearted sad face and she tried to make up by briefly resting her head on my shoulder.

She was a lovely girl with a killer smile, so how could I be annoyed? Since I couldn't speak or read Cantonese or Mandarin, and she spoke no English, I devised a high-tech way to communicate using our phones. By typing English text into a translator app (not Google, as that's not state approved), she would read the Chinese translation. She would type a reply in Chinese on WeChat and I would use the visual translator app to translate into English. Her name was Shen and she was part of the Miao ethnic group of southern China. She worked for a company which cut wood for paper production. Shen showed me a picture of her parent's truck loaded with cut logs, parked up a narrow dirt road in the mountains outside of Nanning.

"Do you drive this truck?" I asked.

"No", she laughed at this idea.

"Do you live in Nanning?"

"I am from here, but don't live here. I return occasionally. Nanning is a shit hole." I hoped my translator app was working correctly, and also intrigued a Chinese equivalent to this English language expression existed.

She gave me her phone number and gestured I should photograph the QR code on her phone. After returning home, I tried to view the QR code, and discovered I had to be invited to join WeChat by a member – the reason why she gave me her phone number. The Chinese are a high-tech race. I read a report where some tech-savvy Chinese beggars now use QR codes to collect money, instead of dealing with the inconvenience of cash.

Three ladies occupied my compartment. This came as no surprise, as gender separation didn't apply in China or Vietnam. In the berth above me lay a woman in her early 40s, already prepared for the night ahead, dressed in her short pink pyjamas. Opposite me sat two Chinese girls named Li Xiu Ying and Liu Yang and both spoke good English. Xiu Ying was a university teacher of home economics (translator app came to the rescue again) and Yang a student.

"What are you studying?" I asked.

"Waste management" she said proudly.

Yang was 24 and they had been friends for 12 years. "We travel everywhere together" she said, but this would be their first trip outside of China. "We have been all over China".

"Have you been to Tibet?" I asked.

"No."

"How about Hong Kong?" I asked, curious to see what her reaction would be to China's 'one country, two systems' policy.

"No, we haven't been there."

"Have you been to Taiwan?"

"No, not yet."

Individual travellers are prohibited from visiting Tibet, and mainland residents can't travel to Taiwan unless they hold a special travel permit. When visiting Hong Kong mainland residents must obtain a Two-way Permit with the appropriate exit endorsement from the Chinese Ministry of Public Security. The applications required to visit these areas may have raised too many questions and perhaps were not worth the trouble.

The girls shared pictures from their phones with me, and I regretted not having more photos on my phone to share back. Although they had a good grasp of English, their vocabulary was limited at times. They didn't understand the word 'vandalism', a concept not widely known or tolerated in China.

The girls tucked into mangosteens, which filled the cabin with a sweet aroma. They also shared a small packet of dried beef with me, which they warned, was HOT. Xiu Yin and Yang watched my reaction and laughed when my eyes began to water. They spoke to each other and at length to the woman above me in a language which didn't quite sound Cantonese or Mandarin. This may have been the local Zhuang dialect.

At 10:20pm our train pulled into Ping Xiang station, by the Vietnamese border, where our carriage attendant instructed us to leave the train with all of our possessions. I was genuinely sorry to leave such an incredible and confusing country, and had experienced nothing but warmth and politeness from those I met.

Exit formalities only took 30 minutes then we were all allowed back on board the train. Another 30 minutes later and our train rolled into the darkness. One hour later the train came to a halt, and an official banged on our compartment door shouting at us all to get off the train.

We had arrived at Dong Dang, on the Vietnamese side of the border. We formed an orderly single line, which snaked out of an unimposing station building, across one track and along our platform.

Border crossings sometimes attract a certain amount of anxiety. As a result, there lacked a sense of urgency, with no pushing or shoving. Come to think of it, I heard no hocking either. Entry formalities into Vietnam took longer compared with Chinese exit formalities, as just one man had been allocated to process an entire trainload of passengers. The immigration officer behind the glass flicked and re-flicked through my passport looking for a Vietnamese visa.

"I don't have a visa as I have a UK passport" I said.

He nodded and stamped my passport. "You must not stay longer than 15 days." he said. He wrote the exit date under the entry stamp and pointed to it.

"You must leave by this date!" he instructed.

"Yes, that's fine."

He returned the passport to me satisfied, and waved me through into Vietnam.

The officers wore their smart, green military-style uniforms, but they did look a bit too large for their smaller frames, as if the Vietnamese Government made 'one size fits all' uniforms which didn't seem to fit anyone at Dong Dang.

Xiu Ying, Yang and I were among the last passengers to be processed. Yang needed to visit the station toilet, so I stood with Xiu Ying and chatted. Ten minutes later her friend still hadn't appeared and all other passengers had now boarded the train. I suggested to Xiu Ying she might want to check if her friend was okay. We didn't want the train to leave unannounced and leave us stranded in Dong Dang.

After what felt like an eternity, they both finally rushed out of the toilet and we all boarded the train. Unfortunately our train lacked a locomotive, so the mild panic was all for nothing. Our Chinese locomotive would be replaced by a Vietnamese one, and that had yet to turn up.

After a wait of 20 minutes, a locomotive rolled into the station and nudged against our waiting carriages. The train lurched and trundled out of the station, 1 hour and 40 minutes after arrival. We had waited as the engine on the late-running northbound Hanoi-Nanning train, would be the same locomotive which would take us back to Hanoi.

DAY 32:
HANOI, VIETNAM

Our train ground to a halt at Ga Gia Lam and went no further, around five kilometres east of the city centre, and on the wrong side of the Red River. In the way sat a rusty, French-built 1902 rail and road bridge. Narrow gauge track crossed the river, whereas the line from the border had been dual gauge, with the Vietnamese narrow and Chinese standard gauges both present. Why had the standard gauge line not continued into the centre of Hanoi? More clearance was needed for larger standard gauge trains, which wasn't possible on the old railway bridge. Also, near the city centre, Vietnamese trains negotiated a stretch of track colloquially called 'Train Street' – a railway line with closely packed houses and shops on either side of the line. As the larger standard gauge rolling stock would pass too close to the buildings, all passengers were kicked off the train at Ga Gia Lam.

I thought about walking the five kilometres into the centre of Hanoi. Once the passengers disembarked from the train and went their separate ways, Gia Lam reverted back to being a quiet and sleepy tropical station.

I needed to get my bearings and be on my way, but I simply couldn't work out which road headed into Hanoi, since no roads looked particularly busy. An older couple was crossing the tracks via a level crossing - the first people seen for around ten minutes.

"Excuse me" I said to the man. "Which road do I take to walk into Hanoi?"

"He doesn't know!" snapped the woman, who decided not to answer on his behalf either, and so my first interaction in Vietnam had been a disappointment.

Based on their age, they may have lived through the Vietnam War, perhaps held a grudge against Americans, and assumed I was one. Either way, the humidity quickly reminded me not to hang around, so returned to the station and found a uniformed man who may have been the station master. In his office, with a cooling fan spinning away on his desk, he showed me a map of Hanoi and explained the route required to walk into the city centre.

Noel Coward once sang about "Mad dogs and Englishmen go out in the midday sun". I was neither a mad dog or an Englishman, so took up the station master's offer of a taxi. He knew a man who could take me into the city centre.

"Does the taxi have a meter?" I asked. Unmetered taxis were a prime source of disoriented tourists being ripped off.

"Yes, it has a meter." he assured me.

After five minutes, the unmetered taxi arrived and I climbed in. Being ripped off when dropped off was a distinct possibility, so when the transaction was completed with no complications, by the front door of the Cosiana Hotel, I was surprised and relieved.

I had requested an early check-in at the Cosiana, as my train would arrive at Ga Gia Lam around 7am, and normal check-in wasn't until after 2pm. Unfortunately the smiling man behind the counter couldn't supply my reserved standard queen-bedded room, which attracted a supplement of 50% of the nightly room rate as an early check-in charge. I had budgeted for this fee, and also anticipated being hot, sticky and tired on arrival after the overnight train from Nanning, so an early check-in would be a much-needed treat.

As the clerk at the desk didn't want to miss out on this extra revenue, he upgraded my room free of charge to a deluxe double. As a result he could accommodate my early check-in and not miss out on the extra 50% fee. This made us both happy.

I received another bonus. Facing a 20-minute wait for a room despite the early check-in, the clerk offered me breakfast, as way of an apology - a treat not normally offered to early check-in guests. The view from the top floor restaurant offered a panoramic view of the city and the railway station and yards below, and all of this while enjoying a free breakfast. I was a happy man.

Once in my room, I unpacked and enjoyed an overdue shower. I had chosen the Cosiana Hotel because of its location, just 200 metres from the main Ga Hanoi station. This is where my train to Ho Chi Minh City would leave from in two days.

I hit the road and in under ten minutes I found myself soaked in sweat due to the heat and humidity. Regular stopovers at cool and shady Buddhist temples, where aromatic incense filled the air, offered some respite and a place to relax. They were also ideal places to escape from the incessant traffic noise. I also found sanctuary in air-conditioned coffee shops and (when desperate) McDonalds, but I could drink only so much iced coffee. Unfortunately consuming too much caffeine results in fatigue and too much coffee results in a need to pee.

I knew the Cosiana sat close to the railway line, but hadn't realised exactly how close. At the northern end of Hanoi Station, just 20 metres from the track, looking out of my bedroom window, I could watch and hear regular diesel locos farting and honking, shunting and generally making a racket. I had hoped to be lulled to sleep by the gentle rumble of passing trains. How wrong I was.

The Cosiana Hotel was located adjacent to a small shop, which sold clocks of all sizes, from alarm clocks to grandfather clocks. The owners lived at the rear of the shop, and I could look out of my bedroom window directly into their back garden area. I first woke at 3:15am thanks to their crowing rooster. It took a well-deserved rest, and started a second crowing session at 4am. Someone shouted at the rooster in Vietnamese encouraging it to shut the fuck up, but the bird failed to comply. Maybe the cock didn't understand Vietnamese.

Eventually the rooster became bored after successfully waking up the entire neighborhood, and now kept quiet, only to be replaced at 5am by the first of the locomotives, which proceeded to fart, honk, shunt and generally make a racket. The locomotives would leave the station platform and stop outside my bedroom, air horns would be given a generous blast, and then reverse back into the station environs.

DAY 33:
HANOI, VIETNAM

Hanoi was a rude awakening to the ways of Vietnam, and I quickly learned a couple of important rules. Pavements aren't for pedestrians, but designed for the parking of motorbikes, and not the clean Chinese electric type, but the stinking petrol variety. Never stop and read a map or phone. Stand still and rickshaw riders and taxi bike drivers will descend from all directions and tout for business. Their ability to spot a tourist was as sharp as a sea gull spotting a dropped French fry. Crossing a road is dangerous. If you cross on a red signal you shall die. Cross on a green signal and you *may* die. Survival odds were still against you, but they improve a little.

If you planned to buy genuine replica designer gear, you were in luck, especially if you wanted North Face or Under Armour. Other brands, like Nike and Adidas, could be found, but you must ask the shop owner for them. Most of the stock, in the middle of summer, catered for winter. The shop owners would earn a higher profit per sale, since jackets and coats were more expensive than a flimsy T-shirt, and after all, if the demand for winter clothing wasn't there, they wouldn't sell these products. If you don't find your preferred brand or colour, just go next door, as all shops sold the same merchandise.

The air was listless and steamy without a hint of a breeze. I continually wiped sweat from my face using my trusty red Paisley patterned bandana, which had a multitude of uses. I was disgusted to discover I could actually wring the sweat out. Even the locals found the heat and humidity a struggle, which was a relief, since I had become a little self-conscious of my appearance. It's not good for the long distance traveller to compromise his foreign street cred by having people point and laugh at you.

I found a rather green and grim looking lake called Ho Hoan Klem.

From here I headed into the adjacent narrow lanes in an area called Hang Gai. How lost could I get in an area of around one square kilometre? Well, after 20 minutes I was still finding out, wandering around this maze looking for an exit.

In one narrow alley a girl of about ten years and her younger brother appeared at a door. She stepped out of her door and said "Hello Mister, How are you?" Perhaps I was on high alert, but the thought of an older foreign man drumming up a conversation with a Vietnamese school-age girl in a strange city made me feel uncomfortable, so I said "Hello" back to her and kept walking. Perhaps I should have talked to her, as looking back, I missed an opportunity to speak to a local, but at the time this felt the right thing to do.

While enjoying the shady lanes of Hang Gai, I spotted a few large rats. I hadn't seen any rats while in China. They must have existed, based on the amount of food available, and would be plump too, but I never actually saw any.

I eventually found my way out of this maze by walking in the direction from where motor scooters were appearing. They had to come from somewhere, so deduced they entered Hang Gai from a main road. This cunning plan worked, and soon surfaced back into the direct sunshine and heat, just north of 'Train Street'. That's what I call 'Zen navigating'. I might not end up where I'd like to go, but I always end up where I needed to be, whether I was aware of it or not.

The best memories were often made when you step outside of your comfort zone.

DAY 34:
DEPART HANOI, VIETNAM

I gave myself plenty of time to catch the Reunification Express from Hanoi to Ho Chi Minh City. Just as well, as the heavens opened up in a tropical downpour upon entering the building. This was another advantage of staying in a hotel just 200 metres from the station.

I found myself alone in a four-berth compartment, and knew this wouldn't last long, although in the back of my mind I foolishly hoped this compartment would be mine all of the way to Ho Chi Minh City.

South of Hanoi, the roads were awash and crowded with slow moving motorbikes, their riders protected by thin, colourful plastic ponchos. Many lanes were submerged, with only the largest vehicles able to cut through the water. Forty minutes from Hanoi, the roads were bone dry.

This train service had frequent stops. In fact the timetable showed 23 intermediate stops between Hanoi and Ho Chi Minh City. Being a single track line, the stations on the timetable not only served passengers, but served as important passing points between trains heading in opposite directions.

We stopped at a quiet, sleepy, tropical station to let a northbound freight train pass, and as the carriage was at the rear of the train, we sat at the extreme end of the station yard. Adjacent to the track lay a chocolate-brown pond, and I studied the surface for signs of life. Small insects danced over the surface of the water. These ponds were used to breed Crucian carp for local consumption. After a few moments a small 'plop' and ripples appeared on the water. That fish would appear in a stew in the near future.

At Ninh Bing, the peace and tranquillity of my empty compartment ended when a party of four filled the three empty berths - occupied by two parents, a daughter of around 12 years, and a young boy of around two years of age. They quickly took over the cabin by sitting on the opposite lower berth and using mine as a footrest. They also closed the door, which denied me a view on the opposite side of the train. The young boy stared into a tablet, watching children's programmes, which featured generous amounts of clapping, singing and American accents. To be honest the parents did a good job keeping the boy occupied, but the relentless Disneyeqsue programmes and their canned laughter began to wear me down. I escaped to the corridor for 30 minutes to enjoy the passing scenery. When I returned to the compartment the boy was still watching his tablet, but the parents were fast asleep.

I tried to do the same. As I lay on my back, with my eyes closed, feeling every lurch of the train on the narrow gauge track below. I also reminded myself how incredibly lucky I was to be experiencing this unique journey.

Later, gazing out of the window, I realised the scenery appeared so... oriental. We passed rice paddies and water buffaloes, and workers hunched over in watery fields wearing lampshade hats. I also spotted the French connection, with numerous Catholic churches and Christian burial grounds.

The family in my compartment left the train at Yen Trung. Our car attendant freshened up the vacated berths by changing the bedding, in preparation for new passengers.

At Dong Le, 437 kilometres from Hanoi, I decided to calculate our progress. In a journey of just 9 hours 15 minutes so far, we had already lost 45 minutes. This didn't look good for the rest of the journey, but being in no hurry, I was more than happy to see the final train journey on this amazing adventure stretched out a few more hours.

I tried to work on my laptop, while ignoring the screaming kids in the corridor, behind my closed compartment door. After an hour, the train ground to a halt at Dong Hoi. The three empty berths were filled by a couple, and also a single woman, who relocated from the adjacent compartment. They were part of a larger group. Another man entered our compartment and decided to sit on my bunk, which was fine assuming the bunk had no bedding in place - a sort of sleeping compartment etiquette. They all started a loud, animated conversation. Having blocked out the screaming kids in the corridor, I knew I was fighting a losing battle. As my metaphysical assimilation had been compromised, I packed the laptop away and just gawked out of the window at the ponds, banana trees and water buffaloes.

Five minutes later they all left to visit the bar at the front end of the train, where they would no doubt partake in several drinks, and return to the compartment to recommence their conversation, but this time even louder. The upholding of the Vietnamese tradition of leaving compartment doors wide open was still alive and well.

Flashes of lightning lit up the dark sky on both sides of the train, and created a silhouette of the hills around us. My first ever overnight sleeper train journey took place many years ago between Singapore and Butterworth, Malaysia. The hills of Northern Vietnam brought back fond memories of a magical, tropical Malaysian train journey. And then my romantic reminisces came to an abrupt end.

An argument broke out in the corridor. A railway employee sat on the floor at the end of the corridor, studying his phone. An angry passenger wanted all of the available windows lowered in an attempt to regulate the increasing temperature in the carriage. According to the digital display at the end of the carriage, the outside temperature was 29°C, and inside 27°C. The conversation, or argument, depending on your point of view, continued for several minutes until the angry man took matters into his own hands and lowered the only two corridor windows which could actually be lowered.

The railway employee fought off interruptions to his mobile phone reading by giving short, disinterested answers. Once the angry passenger returned to his cabin, feeling proud of himself having won a battle against Vietnam Railways, the employee stood up, put his phone in his pocket, and promptly closed the windows again, and walked to the adjoining carriage.

DAY 35:
SOMEWHERE IN SOUTH-CENTRAL VIETNAM

Last night I dreamed of freefalling in an elevator, which may have been due to the tossing and swaying motion of the train on its narrow gauge track. Journeys on narrow gauge trains were rarely smooth, and last night's journey was up there with the worst I had ever experienced. During the early, dark hours of the morning, I heard what sounded like a number of locomotives surrounding our train at a countryside halt. All at once the drivers decided to have a horn blowing competition to see what driver could let rip a blast the longest. This cacophony lasted around ten minutes.

I woke later with the help of a crowing rooster. Was this a flashback to the Cosiana Hotel in Hanoi, when the neighbours damned rooster blasted out a session of crowing at 3am? This loud bird sounded like an Asian rooster - none of your cock-a-doodle-doo nonsense, but a higher pitched kik-kiri-ki sound.

Imagine my disappointment when the first of my travelling companions woke at 5am. By 5:30am everyone had woken and an animated conversation began. Lower berth man enjoyed shouting, despite the close proximity of his companions. To add to the early morning misery, the fourth passenger arrived, and they all entered into a loud conversation about God knows what, with much passion in their voices.

Now fully awake, I discreetly tried to record their conversation on my phone, and translate this using a translation app, as curiosity had gotten the better of me as to what these important debates were about. The fact they jumped straight into their animated topic at sunrise again left me curious. Unfortunately my cunning translator plan didn't work as the background noise, created by our rattling and creaking train, ruined the recording.

Shortly afterwards there were loud voices in the corridor. Our compartment door was still closed and the conversations may have been another loud philosophical discussion about opening windows for ventilation, but deep down I hoped this was a food seller.

I made a quick visit to the toilet, washed and made myself feel semi-presentable. My return to the compartment was blocked by a woman selling black coffee and baguettes. Baguettes? Perhaps a throwback to the French colonial days? The breakfast offer also included three triangles of Laughing Cow cheese. After food and caffeine, my mood improved.

Vietnamese think nothing of standing at your open compartment door and having a good look in. Passengers could be in the middle of an animated debate, be partly dressed or minding their own business, but Vietnamese passengers were happy to stand at the door and study all details available to them. I'll put this down to cultural differences. Also, there seemed to be no hesitation in sitting on the opposite lower berth and using my berth as a footrest while they wore shoes.

Our train pulled into Dui Tri, the first timetable and map reference point of the day, and I calculated we were running 1 hour 8 minutes late. A fifth adult decided to join the fun-four group. He decided to stand at the compartment door, making me a prisoner in my own compartment.

We passed a small forest fire, which burned unattended. This appeared to be one of many recent fires in the hills. The scars showed up as swathes of brown exposed soil amongst the greenery, and older scars, showed signs of green regeneration. As the cleared land wasn't used for cultivation, why had so many fires been lit?

I researched these fires after returning home and discovered this had been a bad year for wild fires in Vietnam. Many fires began accidentally by farmers burning rubbish near forests. Farmers burned tree branches to make space for new trees to grow, but occasionally the fires ran out of control. The burning of incense and joss paper, spread by strong winds, also started fires, exasperated by high temperatures and dry weather.

Group member number five, bored of standing at our compartment door, decided to enter our compartment and sit with his friend who had already made himself comfortable on my berth. Between the heat generated by six passengers in a four-berth cabin and the curtains closed to block out the harsh sunlight (apart from a six inch slit

181

which I insisted on), this was shaping up to be a long ride.

When locals travel on trains, they often pull down window blinds and draw curtains. As far as I was concerned, having travelled halfway around the world to enjoy the scenery, that's what I intended to do. This behaviour wasn't conducive to making friends on trains, but if they close the curtains or blinds, they started it, not me.

The man, who began the argument last night about carriage temperatures, appeared at our compartment door, and moaned to my colleagues. This was obviously still a sore point with him. He pointed at our window, blocked by curtains, and complained these windows couldn't be opened. If he thought the curtain should be fully drawn, he was in for a disappointment, since I hadn't travelled all this way only to look at dusty curtains.

To my great relief, my noisy colleagues all left at Tuy Hoa, where the train arrived 1 hour 5 minutes late. The compartment didn't stay empty for long, being joined by a sole businessman, who said "Good morning.", climbed onto the bunk above me and promptly fell asleep. This gave me the opportunity to work on my laptop for 1½ hours without any distractions.

The children disturbed me just once. Their playing in the corridor came to an abrupt halt when they realised a foreigner was sitting in a compartment using a laptop. They stood by the compartment door and watched me, completely quiet with eyes wide open with amazement, hoping the foreigner would do something entertaining.

One girl sat by my side, and I showed her my videos of the Eiffel Tower and Great Wall of China. The noise of the excited kids in the compartment soon woke the man in the upper berth. He knew a good trick. He offered each child a tub of yogurt to keep them quiet. This cunning plan only worked for a few minutes until the tubs were scraped clean with their plastic spoons.

The kids eventually grew bored with me and returned to the corridor to play. Moments later the food trolley arrived and I snapped up a meal consisting of two skewered pork sausages, pork and beef pieces, a sausage wrapped in seaweed and a sweet potato. Unfortunately the trolley meal service had run out of rice, so while the apologetic woman walked down the corridor and along the train to obtain more rice, her male railway companion made himself comfortable on the opposite, lower berth and played with his phone.

The terminal station of Ga Saigon was located around three kilometres northwest of the city centre. This distance into the city was walkable, but due to the heat and humidity of Southern Vietnam, I decided to jump in a taxi. I still watched the sky, and hoped we wouldn't have a repeat performance of the torrential rain, which marked my departure from Hanoi. Four hours before arrival, the sky had turned cloudy, but the weather remained dry.

Also planning ahead, I realised I had no Vietnamese Dong for the taxi fare. If there were no ATM's at the station, the three kilometre walk to my hotel, in the heat and humidity, might become a reality, if no drivers accepted credit cards.

Southern Vietnam appeared much drier than the north, and featured fruit orchards and almost no banana plants. I watched the passing scenery - palm trees, vineyards and fields of curious dragon fruit, grazing cattle, hay bales and goats galore.

I wondered whether wine was still made in Vietnam, being a former French colony. There may have been a demand for wine back in the day, and could vineyards have survived to the present day? I am no wine connoisseur, but for those who are, the main grape varieties grown in Vietnam are Cardinal and Chambourcin. From 1995 Australian winemakers introduced varieties such as Cabernet Sauvignon and Chardonnay, using land cleared of landmines left over from the Vietnam War. All wines have the same effect on me – I quickly end up drunk and slide under the table, so by sticking to the local beers, I have a fighting chance.

At Thap Cham a mother and daughter occupied the last two berths. As we rolled out of the station, I heard a crowing rooster. At 1:35pm we were too late for a morning wake-up call. The crowing was broadcast from the station speakers! I heard a repeat performance at the following station too, so I knew the rooster the previous night hadn't been imagined. I wasn't going crazy, at least not on this occasion.

The train arrived at Ga Saigon, more or less on time, at 6:38pm. I stepped off the train having completed a train journey of 11,368 miles or 18,296 kilometres from Vila Real de Santo Antonio. I wanted to loiter and savor the moment on the platform, but a uniformed railway staff member seemed keen to discourage this. All passengers were herded across the tracks and into the main station building as quickly as possible.

The only ATM in the station was broken, so decided to try my luck at an information counter.

"Do you speak English?" I asked.

The girl behind the desk glanced up and nodded.

"The ATM over there is broken. Is there anywhere else I can get cash?"

"Are you buying a ticket?"

"No. I need cash for a taxi".

She then proceeded to completely ignore me. Completely.

"I guess that means 'No.' huh?" and I walked out of the station.

Once outside of the station building, I weaved my way through dozens of people who stood around in the humid night air, with taxi touts loitering on the periphery, waiting for customers. Online guides recommended using the green and white Vinasun taxis, as your chances of being ripped off were greatly reduced.

It only took a few seconds before a man in a white shirt approached me and asked "Taxi?"

"Yes, but I don't have cash. Do any drivers take card?"

"Card?"

"Visa? Mastercard?"

The man nodded and walked over to a group of four drivers, talking and smoking. He uttered a few words and they all stopped and looked over in my direction. He returned to me after a few seconds, and motioned for me to jump into a particular Vinasun taxi parked by the kerb.

As Vinasun had a good reputation online, I felt comfortable tossing my backpack into the back of the taxi. Online reports stated traveller's luggage could be held hostage until your new, higher rate was grudgingly paid in full at your destination. No matter what, with just a three-kilometre ride ahead of me, I hoped the fare wouldn't be exorbitant.

The driver swung his taxi onto the busy Cach Mang Thang Tam

thoroughfare and headed into the city centre. We had become part of the nighttime throng of traffic, made up of cars, taxis, vans and farting motor bikes. The meter ticked away, so I sat back, relaxed and enjoyed the night ride through streets of light, noise and humanity.

After what seemed to be a long drive for just three kilometres, the driver pulled up at the narrow All Seasons Hotel. In hindsight, catching a taxi was a good move, since the driver knew exactly where to find the hotel. According to Google Maps, the hotel should have been on the opposite side of the road, and with a narrow shop front and little signage, the All Seasons Hotel would have been a challenge to find.

My double room included a sliding glass door, which led onto a small porch, overlooking a bustling and noisy street below called Le Thanh Ton. I needed no persuasion to have an early night due to the poor night's sleep on the train, but not before the glass doors were shut securely to keep as much of the noise out as possible.

DAY 36:
HO CHI MINH CITY

Farting motorbikes and talking crowds made the road below quite noisy. Directly across the street from the hotel sat the popular Tan Lap restaurant and coffee shop. This seemed to be where most of the chatter came from. I later discovered a second restaurant, also confusingly called Tan Lap, sat adjacent to my hotel. I later learned 'tân lập' was Vietnamese for 'Newly Established'! However, the restaurant across the road displayed this as a huge shop sign, and not some subtle indication as to a change of management. Tan Lap is also the name of a floating village around 100 kilometres west of Ho Chi Minh City. This was the probable source of the name.

The noise finally calmed down after 1am, but a crowing rooster woke me at sunrise. This rooster sounded similar to the crowing rooster, which had haunted me on the overnight train from Hanoi, although to be totally honest, I couldn't tell one rooster from another. Once washed and looking semi-presentable, I stood on the balcony, watched the traffic below, and listened out for the occasional rooster crowing from the Tan Lap restaurant across the road.

As the girl at the hotel reception desk spoke good English, I decided to risk appearing like a complete idiot and talk to her about crowing roosters. She always worked on the day shift, and couldn't ever recall hearing any roosters over the hubbub from the street outside. Alternatively she just wanted to end the conversation as quickly as possible, as talking about roosters with a foreigner possibly left her feeling a little uncomfortable.

I stepped outside, and heard my crowing rooster being broadcast from Tan Lap across the road. After a little research I discovered the rooster brought prosperity and protection. I now understood why Vietnamese Railways and 'Tan Lap' pumped out the sound of a crowing rooster. In Chinese culture the word "rooster" (鸡, jī) had a pronunciation similar to the word for "luck" (吉, jí). As for the crowing rooster behind my hotel room in Hanoi, one day his luck would run out and he would end up in chicken soup.

This morning saw scattered, occasionally heavy, showers. High on my list of things to do was to visit the observation deck of the 258 metre tall Bitexco Financial Tower, which at the time of its construction, was the tallest building in Vietnam. I decided to walk in the general direction of the city, and managed to avoid heavy downpours by nipping into a coffee shop and twice sheltering under dripping shop awnings. Fortunately the sky began to clear, and I reached the tower in a wet shirt, not from rain, but from sweat.

The inspiration for this skyscraper's unique shape came from Vietnam's national flower, the Lotus. Despite being built back in 2010, this structure still received votes as amongst the world's most beautiful skyscraper designs. A helipad, which jutted out from the 52nd floor, added to the building's 'coolness'. Bitexco Group, a Vietnamese multi-industry corporation, focussed on real estate development. What better way to advertise your business than with a helipad attached to your HQ.

From the observation deck the view highlighted the importance of the city's location as a river port. The brown Saigon River snaked through the region as far as the eye could see. Many areas of Ho Chi Minh City had avoided redevelopment. These neighbourhoods were characterised by single storey buildings and criss-crossed by narrow lanes, similar to the maze at Hang Gai in Hanoi, where I managed to briefly misplace myself three days ago.

For the last 34 days I had carried a piece of granite ballast from the start of the line at the Vila Real de Santo Antonio buffer stop. I planned to carry this stone all the way to Ho Chi Minh City where it would be dropped onto the track by the buffer stop at the other end. This would be a symbolic gesture of the journey. However, I still needed to complete this task and try and access the buffer 150 metres beyond the end of the platform at Ga Saigon. When the train arrived into Ho Chi Minh City last night, the end of the railway yard was hidden in darkness, so unfortunately I couldn't make a quick dash to the end of the line. Uniformed staff quickly ushered passengers off the platforms, discouraging any loitering by crazy British tourists.

I returned to my hotel to freshen up, and then ordered a Grab motor bike. The thought of clinging on the back of a zippy motor bike

187

as it swerved through the manic city traffic of Ho Chi Minh City hit me as a really good idea. I didn't have a Grab app set up on my phone, so the nice girl at the hotel reception desk ordered one for me. Still concerned about my fascination with roosters, she perhaps thought it safer to comply. ("Oh no, it's that foreigner with the rooster fixation again.") This bike ride turned out to be an exhilarating experience. As I waved my driver away at Ga Saigon, I wondered whether such a journey would have been included under my travel insurance.

Ga Saigon was quiet and had a sleepy tropical feel about it; the exact opposite of the organised chaos of last night. A few people sat in the relative coolness of the waiting area, and although shops and kiosks were open, they had no customers.

Uniformed officials manned all the entrances onto the platform. Perhaps Vietnam Railways had been tipped off a crazy Brit would attempt an eccentric stunt, or keeping passengers off platforms was normal practice. Imagine my disappointment. I visualised many times the walk along the track to the buffer stop to complete the ballast dropping ceremony. I even carried a short explanation as to what I was up to, printed off in Vietnamese, courtesy of Google translate, on the off-chance an official barked at me as I walked along the tracks. However, approaching a gate guard and showing him my printed translation would have only achieve confused looks and a sharp rebuking. It's easier to beg for forgiveness than ask for approval. That way your task was completed without waiting for permission which can be time consuming and often wasn't even granted. It was time for Plan B.

I walked along the outside of the station and found a long, cream coloured, one storey building. On the front of the building a sign which read "trạm vận chuyển hàng hóa" which translated meant "freight station." This street had been checked on Google Street View before leaving home. I remembered how the street and building appeared and what my cunning plan of action would be, without any loitering or indecision, which may have attracted unwanted attention. The sight of a disoriented foreigner entering this area may have aroused more suspicion than one entering the station platform past a uniformed guard.

I also checked for access points from a nearby street. One shop had an adjacent alleyway, which led through to the freight yard behind, and my buffer stop. This green building belonged to Sai Gon Ha Noi Transport Packaging Company Limited. The freight yard was visible through the alleyway, but two chatting men blocked my access. The thought of a foreigner strolling through this alleyway would have caused a high degree of suspicion and my plan would have failed.

Defeated, I brought the lump of Portuguese granite home and it became an unusual souvenir of my remarkable journey. The stone now sits on a wooden block with a brass plaque attached on the front. I had completed the longest continuous train journey in the world and, to be honest, I was glad it was over. Don't get me wrong. I would love to repeat the journey, perhaps in reverse, and maybe in winter instead of the middle of a sticky summer. However I was still glad the journey was over, because it had been hard work.

There had been no serious delays, didn't end up lost, wasn't arrested, and experienced no serious problems at border crossings. I had a spot of Siberian Squits across Mongolia and on arrival in Beijing, but otherwise no health problems at all. I met unforgettable people, saw unforgettable sights and the food was amongst the best I had ever tasted.

Back at the All Seasons Hotel, I freshened up for my last night and meal in Vietnam. Sadly, most restaurants were closed, with their shutters securely pulled down. Peering along one narrow street I spotted a row of busy restaurants, complete with tables and chairs spilling out onto the street itself. Motor cyclists weaved their bikes around other bikes and pedestrians, making slow progress. "This is more like it." I thought. "This will be good." I found an empty table with a plastic, red tartan tablecloth, sat down and studied the menu.

My order arrived quickly and I started working my way through the vegetarian spring rolls, and sipped my Tiger beer. I heard a few English language conversations near me - an Australian accent nearby, and a South African accent further along, and discreetly observed the diners. Many of the couples were bored Vietnamese girls, and middle-aged Caucasian men. There seemed to be little chemistry between the couples. The men drank their beer, and seemed to engage in little conversation. In fact the girls conversed with other bored girls sitting nearby, while their partners guzzled from bottles of Tiger.

What did Vietnamese women get out of a relationship with Western men? From the viewpoint of a heterosexual male, I could definitely see one side of the equation. One online report suggested roughly 10,000 marriages took place between Vietnamese and foreigners each year. Around 92% were of a Vietnamese woman marrying a foreign male and it explained probable reasons. The first reason suggested the woman's greatest duty was to help their parents escape a life of extreme poverty. The promise of material comforts also played an important part.

Vietnamese traditional culture expected women to be nurturing, willing to sacrifice and serve their men. Many Vietnamese men, as a result, were seen to be lazy. A husband from a different culture removed much of the pressure off their shoulders.

Vietnamese women found marriage to a foreign man easier, being less judgmental about their partner's past, and whose family did not need to give approval of the marriage. Foreign men placed no restrictions on their bride's career, education, family background or virginity.

There was a curiosity about the world outside of Vietnam. Marrying a foreign man generally opened up opportunities to travel and experience cultural differences and open the door to potential life changing opportunities.

And of course, there was love, which crossed international boundaries. I just didn't see a lot of love in this narrow, busy street in Ho Chi Minh City.

I lay in bed with a full belly and the disappointment of this being my last night in Vietnam. I thought about the thin, black line I ran my finger along, in a school atlas, over 40 years earlier. At the time such a journey seemed too complicated to complete. There were too many visas to arrange, too many border crossings and too many communist countries, which regarded Westerners as troublesome and inconvenient.

I may not be able to recall one single fact from Silas Marner, but I could tell you a story or two about foreign cultures and the joy of human diversity.

It then occurred to me – how do I get home now?